Pentateuch Illuminated

A Five Part Series Introducing

A New American Scripture—
How and Why the Real Illuminati™ Created
The Book of Mormon

Pentateuch Illuminated

A Five Part Series Introducing

A New American Scripture—
How and Why the Real Illuminati™ Created
The Book of Mormon

The Real Illuminati

Worldwide United Publishing Large Print
Melba, Idaho

Pentateuch Illuminated: A Five Part Series Introducing *A New American Scripture—How and Why the Real Illuminati™ Created the Book of Mormon*

Text and cover design copyright © 2020 by Worldwide United Publishing

April 6, 2020
First Edition

The text of this Large Print edition is unabridged. Other aspects of the book may vary. Set in 18 pt. Baskerville.

LARGE PRINT HARDBACK ISBN 978-1-937390-29-7

Worldwide United Publishing
an imprint of Pearl Publishing, LLC
2587 Southside Blvd., Melba, ID 83641
www.pearlpublishing.net—1.888.499.9666

CONTENTS

Introduction

Pentateuch Illuminated is a presentation of information taken from the notes that were provided to the publisher's editors. These notes were arranged and taken from the preliminary rough draft that we (the Real Illuminati™) provided to the publisher.

Pentateuch Illuminated introduces the second book in our Trilogy, *A New American Scripture—How and Why the Real Illuminati™ Created the Book of Mormon.*

We've instructed the publisher to release this prelude to our second book in order to provide the reader with an overall and clear preview. We hope this preview will enhance the reader's ability to understand the intent of the second book of our Trilogy. This five-part series is taken from the notes that we have accumulated in preparation to publish this second book.

At the present time, we have not designated a definitive timeframe for the publication of the second book of our Trilogy. We hope that the sincere researcher of Real Truth will take the time and effort to thoroughly study *Pentateuch Illuminated*. It can be used as a study guide. It provides a preemptive overview of what we hope will finally put to rest any doubt about why our new American scripture, *the Book of Mormon*, was created and published in 1830.

If we were asked to explain the purpose of our new American scripture in one sentence, that sentence would be:

The intent of writing our new American scripture was to dissuade the perpetuation of, and to end, organized religion and poverty.

For the Intent to Do Good

Part One

If you haven't read our new American scripture (known as the *Book of Mormon*)[1] or its addendum *The Sealed Portion—The Final Testament of Jesus Christ*,[2] you have no right to judge our writings, or our intent in writing them. Without reading either yourself, you do not have the ability to judge either book properly. And without reading either, how is possible to speculate on *why* we wrote them?

Nor should our writings be judged by the actions of those who improperly use them and transfigure their meaning and intent. There are religions that have developed from using our writings. None of the modern Mormon sects that have incorporated our new American scripture into their religious organization has used it for the intent or purpose for which it was written. The people

---

[1] "The Book of Mormon," *Real Illuminati*™, accessed March 29, 2020, https://www.realilluminati.org/the-book-of-mormon. This version is the original 1830 version. (Hereafter referred to as *BOM*; verses were later added.)

[2] *The Sealed Portion—The Final Testament of Jesus Christ*, trans. Christopher, 2nd ed. (Worldwide United, 2008), https://www.realilluminati.org/the-sealed-portion/. (Hereafter referred to as *TSP*.)

who believe that the *Book of Mormon* is another "word of God" comparable to the Bible are generally called "Mormons." The modern Church of Jesus Christ of Latter-day Saints (LDS/Mormon Church)[3] is the largest sect of Mormons. Nothing this religion does or pretends to do is consistent with our *Book of Mormon*.

As early as 1959, the modern LDS/Mormon Church publicly proclaimed its purpose and goals (*its* intent):

> [I]n all of its activities, a quorum of the Priesthood must keep in mind the threefold duty which rests upon the Church, namely: To keep the members of the Church in the way of their full duty. To teach the Gospel to those who have not yet heard it or accepted it. To provide for the dead, through the ordinances of the temple, the means by which the dead, if obedient, may participate in the blessings

---

[3] "The Church of Jesus Christ of Latter-day Saints," *Wikipedia, The Free Encyclopedia*, last modified April 1, 2020, https://en.wikipedia.org/wiki/The_Church_of_Jesus_Christ_of_Latter-day_Saints.

that are enjoyed by those who have won citizenship in the Kingdom of God.[4]

<u>Nothing</u> in our writings (new American scripture) <u>supports</u> these first three <u>LDS</u>/Mormon mission statements: to preach the <u>gospel</u>, perfect the <u>Saints,</u> and <u>redeem the dead.</u>[5] In fact, our new American scripture presents an entirely different "fulness of the everlasting Gospel ... as delivered by the Savior to the ancient inhabitants"[6] than what is taught by the Mormons.

Our writings <u>condemn Mormon genealogy efforts</u>[7] aimed at finding the names of one's ancestors and submitting these names to the LDS/Mormon Church. LDS members do this so that Mormon "saving ordinances"[8] can

---

[4] John A. Widtsoe, *Priesthood and Church Government* (Salt Lake City: Deseret Book, 1939), 152.

[5] "Remember the Mission of the Church," *The Church of Jesus Christ of Latter-day Saints*, April 3, 1982, https://www.churchofjesuschrist.org/study/general-conference/1982/04/remember-the-mission-of-the-church.

[6] *See The Pearl of Great Price* (Salt Lake City: The Church of Jesus Christ of Latter-day Saints, 2013), Joseph Smith—History, 1:34. (Hereafter referred to as *PGP* and *JSH*.)

[7] "FamilySearch," *The Church of Jesus Christ of Latter-day Saints*, accessed April 2, 2020, https://www.familysearch.org/en/.

[8] "Ordinances," *The Church of Jesus Christ of Latter-day Saints*, accessed March 29, 2020, https://www.churchofjesuschrist.org/study/manual/gospel-topics/ordinances.

be vicariously done for the dead.[9] Genealogy is condemned in our *Book of Mormon*.[10] Genealogy research supports baptism for the dead (those who "die without law").[11] Mormons erroneously believe that anyone who dies without receiving Mormon religious priesthood ordinances are damned.[12] Vicarious (posthumous)[13] work on behalf of the "those who die without law" is not mentioned in our *Book of Mormon*, but is actually condemned. These "vain oblations"[14] have replaced the "intent to do good"[15] meant by the overall message our new American scripture.

---

[9] Russel[l] M. Nelson, "Vicarious Work for the Dead," *The Church of Jesus Christ of Latter-day Saints*, October 8, 2006, https://www.churchofjesuschrist.org/media-library/video/2012-06-2710-vicarious-work-for-the-dead.

[10] Joseph Smith, Junior, Author and Proprietor. *The Book of Mormon—An Account Written by the Hand of Mormon, Upon Plates Taken from the Plates of Nephi* (Palmyra: E. B. Grandin, 1830), 16. (*BOM*, 1 Nephi, chapter 6.)

[11] *BOM*, Moroni 8:22.

[12] "Baptisms for the Dead," *The Church of Jesus Christ of Latter-day Saints*, accessed April 5, 2020, https://www.churchofjesuschrist.org/study/manual/gospel-topics/baptisms-for-the-dead.

[13] Definition: "Given to someone after their death, or happening after their death." *See* "posthumous" in *Macmillan English Dictionary*, accessed April 4, 2020, https://www.macmillandictionary.com/dictionary/american/posthumous#posthumous_3.

[14] *King James Bible*, Isaiah 1:13. The full context of Isaiah chapter 1 was included in the *Book of Mormon's* original manuscript. *See* Christopher, *Without Disclosing My True Identity—The Authorized and Official Biography of the Mormon Prophet, Joseph Smith, Jr.* (Melba: Worldwide United, 2012), 287. (Hereafter referred to as *JS Bio*.)

[15] *BOM*, Jacob 2:19.

After Joseph Smith, Jr.[16] (the alleged first leader of Mormonism) was killed, the early church members were in confusion and disarray. Two main groups emerged from the battle over priesthood succession and control: 1) the *Church of Jesus Christ of Latter-day Saints* and 2) the *Reorganized Church of Jesus Christ of Latter Day Saints* (now known as the *Community of Christ*).[17] The former was led by Brigham Young[18] and was pro-plural marriage. The latter, led by Joseph's closest companions and his immediate family, were vehemently *against* plural marriage. Contrary to modern historical subjectivism[19] (belief), largely based on Brigham Young's heavily edited

---

[16] Read *Without Disclosing My True Identity—The Authorized and Official Biography of the Mormon Prophet, Joseph Smith, Jr.* https://www.realilluminati.org/without-disclosing-my-true-identity. *See also* "Joseph Smith," *Wikipedia, The Free Encyclopedia*, last modified March 26, 2020, https://en.wikipedia.org/wiki/Joseph_Smith.

[17] "Community of Christ," *Wikipedia, The Free Encyclopedia*, last modified January 20, 2020, https://en.wikipedia.org/wiki/Community_of_Christ.

[18] "Brigham Young," *Wikipedia, The Free Encyclopedia*, last modified March 25, 2020, https://en.wikipedia.org/wiki/Brigham_Young.

[19] Definition of subjective: "Based on your own feelings and ideas and not on facts." *See* "subjective (adjective)," in *Merriam-Webster Dictionary*, accessed April 6, 2020, https://www.merriam-webster.com/dictionary/subjective.

version of *Church* History,[20] Joseph's intimates were well aware that he detested polygamy, in all of its forms.

The Mormon religion shows uncanny similarities to the Muslim religion, where Sunni and Shia adherents fight among themselves over proper ecclesiastical succession order. The Mormon sect that developed under Brigham Young and relocated to Utah believed that succession properly belonged to Joseph Smith's closest disciples. This reflects the comparable Sunni idea. The opposing group, represented by the *Reorganized* Church, believed that succession belonged to Joseph Smith's family line (similar to the Shia idea).[21] (For more information on these two major religions' similarities, read *The True History of Religion—How Religion Destroys the Human Race and What the Real Illuminati™ Has Attempted to do Through Religion to Save the Human Race.*)[22]

---

[20] B. H. Roberts, *History of the Church of Jesus Christ of Latter-day Saints. An Introduction and notes by B. H. Roberts. Seven Volumes* (Salt Lake City: Deseret Book, 1980). Nicknamed *Documentary History of the Church* or *DHC*, https://archive.org/details/HistoryOfTheChurchhcVolumes1-7original1902EditionPdf/mode/2up.

[21] "Shia Islam," *Wikipedia, The Free Encyclopedia*, last modified March 29, 2020, https://en.wikipedia.org/wiki/Shia_Islam.

[22] Referred to as *THOR* (Melba: Worldwide United, 2019), written by the same authors as this book (The Real Illuminati™). *See specifically* pages 224–8, 231–6 (large print edition) on this topic, https://www.realilluminati.org/the-true-history-of-religion.

Brigham Young's Mormons, who had moved out west to Utah after the death of Joseph Smith, eventually disavowed the practice of polygamy in order to get along with the rest of the United States of America. However, LDS/Mormons today still believe that plural marriage is a Celestial principle that will be lived during the millennial reign of their Christ,[23] and also after life, if one gains entrance into the Mormon Celestial Kingdom (God's highest degree of Glory).

Astoundingly, our *Book of Mormon* condemns plural marriage as a "gross crime," … "which thing [is] abominable before … the Lord."[24]

As briefly mentioned above, exposing the most glaring hypocrisy of the Church of all, our *Book of Mormon* condemns "redeeming the dead"[25] as an abomination. Our

---

[23] *See* Bruce R. McConkie, "Polygamy," in *Mormon Doctrine*, 2nd ed. (Salt Lake City: Bookcraft, 1966), 410, https://archive.org/details/MormonDoctrine1966/page/n413/mode/2up. "The holy practice will commence again after the Second Coming of the Son of Man and the ushering in of the millennium."

[24] *BOM*, Jacob 2:22–35.

[25] "Redemption of the Dead," *The Church of Jesus Christ of Latter-day Saints*, accessed April 1, 2020, https://www.churchofjesuschrist.org/study/manual/foundations-of-the-restoration-teacher-material-2019/lesson-19-class-preparation-material-redemption-of-the-dead.

new American scripture is clear that those who do work for the dead "are in danger of death, hell, and an endless torment."[26] ("The dead" whom the LDS/Mormons do temple work for refers to those who "die without the law."[27] These do not need baptism or to be redeemed!)[28]

The above obvious contradictions, as well as many others, will be presented in the details that we provide throughout *A New American Scripture—How and Why the Real Illuminati™ Created the Book of Mormon*.

Needless to say, our intended "Lord"[29] and God (the god of the *Book of Mormon*) is extremely different from the LDS/Mormon Lord and God, a God who appears to completely ignore His own holy word. In 1842, we left instructions for Joseph Smith to present what he knew (the Real Truth), but never revealed to his followers, through the presentation of a symbolic play. During the play, it is

See also Richard G. Scott, "The Joy of Redeeming the Dead," *The Church of Jesus Christ of Latter-day Saints*, October 7, 2012, https://www.churchofjesuschrist.org/study/general-conference/2012/10/the-joy-of-redeeming-the-dead.

[26] *BOM*, Moroni 8:21.

[27] *BOM*, Moroni 8:22.

[28] *BOM*, Moroni, chapter 8, especially verse 22. *See also BOM*, Alma 1:4;

[29] *BOM*, Jacob 2:24.

clearly presented that *all* Mormons are following and receiving revelation and answers to their prayers *only* from the "god of this world."[30]

In our play, the character *Lucifer* is the only god that has anything to do with people while humans go through mortality upon Earth (the "lone and dreary world.") Although presented in symbolism to avoid further persecution from his critics and enemies (most of whom were past followers and supporters), the information Joseph Smith tried to deliver to his deceived followers in 1842 was clear: *Elohim* and *Jehovah* have nothing to do with mortals during their mortal sojourn. The only god that hears and answers prayers is *Lucifer*, "the god of this world."[31]

The plates from which our writings allegedly came contained two parts. The first part (1/3) is known as the *Book of Mormon*. The second portion (2/3) was said to

---

[30] *See* Christopher, *Sacred, not Secret—The [Authorized and] Official Guide In Understanding the LDS Temple Endowment* (Melba: Worldwide United, 2008), 85–113, https://www.realilluminati.org/sacred-not-secret. (Hereafter referred to as *Sacred, not Secret* or *SNS*.) *See also JS Bio*, 547.

[31] *SNS*, 88.

contain the "greater portion of the word."[32] This is known as *The Sealed Portion.* After publishing *The Sealed Portion* of the *Book of Mormon* (2004), the LDS/Mormon Church was forced to amend its public mission statement.[33] A proper and honest investigation will uncover the fact that this occurred due to our efforts and the release of our book's 2/3 sealed portion.[34]

The intent of our *Book of Mormon* was to impress upon the religiously based mind that caring for the poor and needy was the most important part of any religious endeavor. We knew that there was a high probability that the early American Christians would reject the real intent of our scripture and form a religion based on everything *except* administering to the needs of the poor. Knowing of this great likelihood, we incorporated within the storyline the idea that the *sealed portion* was far greater and more important than the *unsealed portion* that was published as

---

[32] *BOM*, Alma 12:10.

[33] Peggy Fletcher Stack, "New LDS emphasis: Care for the needy," *The Salt Lake Tribune*, December 9, 2009, https://archive.sltrib.com/story.php?ref=/lds/ci_13965607.

[34] *See* Christopher, "Letter to The First Presidency of the Church of Jesus Christ of Latter-day Saints," in *TSP* (Worldwide United, 2008), 596–7, www.pearlpublishing.net/tsp/download/TSP_Secured.pdf.

the *Book of Mormon*. In essence, our *sealed portion* was an intended *failsafe* incorporated into the storyline in case our "intent to do good" was ignored.

Upon reading *The Sealed Portion—The Final Testament of Jesus Christ,* many faithful members have left that Church. They began to realize how far off course that Church had taken the intent of our writings. Online blogs began to discuss the differences between *our* intent to do good, and their Church's three-fold mission, which didn't include anything about taking care of the poor.

Reading her story started my new journey.

Ida Smith[35] was a very prominent Mormon and a direct descendant of Hyrum Smith.[36] Hyrum was killed alongside his younger brother, Joseph. After Ida read our books, she began to confront the highest leaders of the LDS/Mormon Church and a few other powerful politicians (also her good friends) about their hypocrisy. It was then that, *miraculously*, the Mormon God announced an addition to

---

[35] "The Man From Joe's Bar and Grill, The Autobiography of Christopher Marc Nemelka," *Real Illuminati™*, accessed April 2, 2020, https://www.realilluminati.org/the-man-from-joe-s-bar-and-grill.

[36] *JS Bio*, 15–17. *See also* "Hyrum Smith," *Wikipedia, The Free Encyclopedia*, last modified December 13, 2019, https://en.wikipedia.org/wiki/Hyrum_Smith.

this church's original three-part mission statement that included caring for the poor and needy.[37]

We gave a prophecy in our *Book of Mormon* about modern-day religions, that "all churches" do what they do "to become popular in the eyes of the world."[38] True to this prophecy, the modern Mormon/LDS "God" has a history of changing long-standing church doctrine and policy so that the Church looks good and is more acceptable to the world.

In 1890, polygamy was interfering with the Mormon's chance for statehood from the United States Supreme Court. Because of this, and under threat of loss of its political rights and properties,[39] the Mormon practice of plural marriage ended by "way of revelation."[40] However, as mentioned above, many LDS/Mormons continue to

---

[37] Stack, "New LDS emphasis." *See also* Chris Henrichsen, "A New Mission: Caring for the Poor and the Needy," *Faith-Promoting Rumor* (blog), December 6, 2009, http://faithpromotingrumor.com/2009/12/06/a-new-mission-caring-and-the-poor-and-the-needy.

[38] *BOM*, 1 Nephi 22:23.

[39] Dennis Lythgoe, "Utah Statehood," *Deseret News*, February 8, 1996, https://www.deseret.com/1996/2/8/19223925/utah-statehood.

[40] *See* "Official Declaration—1" (October 6, 1890) in *The Doctrine and Covenants of The Church of Jesus Christ of Latter-day Saints* (Salt Lake City: The Church of Jesus Christ of Latter-day Saints, 1986), 291, https://www.churchofjesuschrist.org/study/scriptures/dc-testament/od/1. (Hereafter referred to as *D&C*.)

believe (although in secret, because it is not popular in the "eyes of the world")[41] that plural marriage will be reinstituted upon Earth during the millennial reign of *their* Christ and God, and in Eternity.[42]

In 1978—again under pressure to gain popularity in the eyes of the world—the Mormon doctrine that did not allow black people to hold the LDS priesthood ended by "way of revelation."[43]

Disturbing to us (the Real Illuminati™), the Mormon Lord and God also commands changes[44] to our 1842 play[45] whenever it is seen unfavorably "in the eyes of the world."[46]

As was briefly mentioned above, shortly before Joseph Smith was murdered in 1844, we authorized him to present

---

[41] *BOM*, 1 Nephi 22:23.

[42] "Mormonism and polygamy," *Wikipedia, The Free Encyclopedia*, last modified March 31, 2020, https://en.wikipedia.org/wiki/Mormonism_and_polygamy. "The LDS Church today teaches that plural marriage can only be practiced when specifically authorized by God. According to this view, the 1890 Manifesto and Second Manifesto rescinded God's prior authorization given to Joseph Smith. …In the case where a man's first wife dies, and the man remarries, and both of the marriages involve a sealing, LDS authorities teach that in the afterlife, the man will enter a polygamous relationship with both wives."

[43] *D&C*, "Official Declaration—2" (June 1, 1978).

[44] "Timeline," *ldsendowment.org*, accessed April 6, 2020, http://www.ldsendowment.org/timeline.html.

[45] *Sacred, not Secret*, https://www.realilluminati.org/sacred-not-secret.

[46] *BOM*, 1 Nephi 22:23.

some Real Truths (i.e., "mysteries of God")[47] in symbolism. These ideas were presented as a play in 1842 that has now became known as the LDS *Temple Endowment* presentation.[48] Joseph often told his followers that he was not explaining things as they *really* were, because if he did, they might "rise up and kill [him]."[49] Had Joseph explained everything that he knew in plainness, he would have been killed sooner than he was.

Again, our 1842 play reveals the Real Truth through allegorical presentations and clearly explains which god we know is leading the LDS/Mormon Church, as well as all other religions: It is the god of this world,[50] "Lucifer," a character in our play who was meant to represent mortal pride and ego.[51] All religious belief, of any kind, is the result of human pride and ego. This will be explained thoroughly in our book, *A New American Scripture*, along with how we

---

[47] *BOM*, Alma 12:10.

[48] "About the Temple Endowment," *The Church of Jesus Christ of Latter-day Saints*, accessed April 5, 2020, https://www.churchofjesuschrist.org/temples/what-is-temple-endowment.

[49] As recalled by Parley P. Pratt, "Reminiscences of the Church in Nauvoo," *Millennial Star* 55, no. 36 (September 4, 1893): 585.

[50] *See SNS*, Chapter 5, "The God of this World," 85–113.

[51] *SNS*, 49.

used the religious concept of good ("God") and evil ("the devil") to illustrate how easily people are deceived and controlled by unscrupulous religious leaders.

During one scene of our original play, the character representing a True Messenger confronts the character playing Lucifer (mortal pride and ego) and asks, "How is your religion received by this community?"[52]

The play's director (Joseph Smith, Jr.) instructed the True Messenger actor to specifically look at and gesture toward the LDS/Mormon people in the audience (those who were viewing the play) when he asked that question.[53] The Lucifer character was then instructed to look directly at the audience and respond, "Very well, excepting this man. He does not seem to believe anything we preach."[54]

The "excepting this man" phrase refers to the Adam character, who was very confused by the preaching of Lucifer's religious minister. The minister character (actor) was a main character in the original play. That character

---

[52] *See JS Bio*, 535–6. *See also SNS*, 105.
[53] *JS Bio*, 547.
[54] *SNS*, 105.

was removed by LDS/Mormon leaders circa 1990.[55] Of course, it was removed "by way of commandment" through revelation received from the LDS/Mormon Lord and God.[56]

The intent of our original play was to portray ALL religions as products of *Lucifer's* deception (the human nature of pride and ego), led by religious leaders (represented by the Minister character). We especially intended to portray this about the religion that had developed into the LDS/Mormon Church (the community of Mormons that developed in and around Nauvoo, Illinois by 1842, and which was eventually reestablished by Brigham Young in Utah).[57] Because this crucial part did not sit well with the "eyes of the world,"[58] Mormon leaders

---

[55] "The LDS Endowment," *ldsendowment.org*, accessed March 29, 2020, http://www.ldsendowment.org/paralleltelestial.html.

See also John Dart, "Mormons Modify Temple Rites: Ceremony: Woman's vow to obey husband is dropped. Changes are called most significant since 1978," *Los Angeles Times*: May 5, 1990, https://www.latimes.com/archives/la-xpm-1990-05-05-vw-353-story.html.

[56] "Prophets have taught that there will be no end to such adjustments as directed by the Lord to His servants." As quoted from "First Presidency Statement on Temples (Official Statement)," *The Church of Jesus Christ of Latter-day Saints*, January 2, 2019, https://newsroom.churchofjesuschrist.org/article/temple-worship.

See also "Background surrounding the 1990 changes to the Mormon temple ceremony," *lds-mormon.com*, accessed April 2, 2020, http://www.lds-mormon.com/whytemplechanges.shtml.

[57] "Brigham Young," *Wikipedia*.

[58] *BOM*, 1 Nephi 22:23.

removed the character and all of the lines associated with this character. They also removed many other parts of our original play's presentation[59] that they felt would make their church unpopular in the "eyes of the world."

Some of the prophecies we created and incorporated into our new American scripture's storyline were meant to describe modern-day religions and include what the purpose of these religions would be:

> to get gain, to get power over the flesh, to become popular in the eyes of the world, and seek the lusts of the flesh and the things of the world.[60]

It was obviously **not** *our* intent to be "popular in the eyes of the world" when we dressed the *Lucifer* character in our play in a Masonic apron. It was the same type of apron that the most popular Founding Father of the United States (George Washington) wore when he laid the

---

[59] *Sacred, not Secret*, https://www.realilluminati.org/sacred-not-secret.
[60] *BOM*, 1 Nephi 22:23.

cornerstone for the U.S. Capitol Building[61]—that "great and spacious building"[62] that would establish the laws for the United States of America.

Nevertheless, if the intent of a religious god **is**

to get gain, to get power over the flesh, to become popular in the eyes of the world, and seek the lusts of the flesh and the things of the world,[63]

then the LDS/Mormon Church has achieved its God's goals![64]

In our new scripture, we warned the Americans about their religions. We presented Americans as being "lifted up in the pride of their hearts."[65] Our warnings have gone

[61] "United States Capitol," *Wikipedia, The Free Encyclopedia*, last modified March 29, 2020, https://en.wikipedia.org/wiki/United_States_Capitol.

[62] *BOM*, 1 Nephi 11:36.

[63] *BOM*, 1 Nephi 22:23.

[64] Stacy Johnson, "President Trump meets with LDS Church leadership at Welfare Square," *Daily Herald*, December 4, 2017, https://www.heraldextra.com/news/local/faith/president-trump-meets-with-lds-church-leadership-at-welfare-square/article_f049d6bd-7fff-5607-af43-2129af49b535.html;

"City Creek Center Opens," *The Church of Jesus Christ of Latter-day Saints*, March 22, 2012, https://newsroom.churchofjesuschrist.org/article/city-creek-center-an-economic-revitalization;

Caroline Winter, Katherine Burton, Nick Tamasi and Anita Kumar, "The money behind the Mormon message," *Bloomberg Businessweek*, October 5, 2012, *The Salt Lake Tribune*, https://archive.sltrib.com/article.php?id=54478720&itype=cmsid.

[65] *BOM*, Jacob 2:13; Alma 4:8; 3 Nephi 16:10; Mormon 8:28, 36.

unheeded. The Americans who accept/ed our new scripture embrace a prideful belief that their religion is the "only true and living church of God on Earth,"[66] "even to the envying of them who belong to their churches."[67]

Mormons envy positions of authority and leadership in their church, more so than any other religion on Earth. A lay (ordinary) member of this church can become a Bishop, a Stake President, or even a General Authority. Men especially covet (envy) holding one of these positions. They do everything they are told to do so that they might be chosen to become a leader or teacher in this corrupt religion.

Knowing that the Americans might corrupt, transfigure, and misuse our new scripture, we warned them, asking:

<u>Why have ye transfigured the holy word of God?[68]</u>

---

[66] Dallin H. Oaks, "The Only True and Living Church," *The Church of Jesus Christ of Latter-day Saints*, June 25, 2010, https://www.churchofjesuschrist.org/study/new-era/2011/08/the-only-true-and-living-church;

Henry B. Eyring, "The True and Living Church," *The Church of Jesus Christ of Latter-day Saints*, April 5, 2008, https://www.churchofjesuschrist.org/study/general-conference/2008/04/the-true-and-living-church.

[67] *BOM*, Mormon 8:28.

[68] *BOM*, Mormon 8:33.

The Mormons have completely ignored our intent for writing a new American scripture. Joseph Smith warned his early followers that:

> they have strayed from mine ordinances, and have broken mine everlasting covenant; They seek not the Lord to establish his righteousness, but every man walketh in his own way, and after the image of his own god, whose image is in the likeness of the world, and whose substance is that of an idol.[69]

> Which vanity and unbelief have brought the whole church under condemnation. And this condemnation resteth upon the children of Zion, even all. And they shall remain under this condemnation until they repent and remember the new covenant, even the *Book of Mormon* and

---

[69] *D&C*, 1:15–16.

the former commandments which I have given them, not only to say, but to do according to that which I have written.[70]

In our new scripture, we present the result of this image, vanity, and pride as the "great and abominable church of the devil."[71] As mentioned above, in our play we name the character that represents the devil: *Lucifer.*[72] (This play is explained in detail in our book titled *Sacred, not Secret—The [Authorized and] Official Guide In Understanding the LDS Temple Endowment.*)[73]

"Lucifer" represents the vanity and pride that entices our ego. Our play's Eve character represents the *Ego* part of the human psyche.[74] This three-part cognitive setup of the human psyche[75] is often described as the *Superego* (Adam), *Ego*

---

[70] *D&C*, 84:55–87.

[71] *See BOM*, 1 Nephi, chapters 13–14.

[72] *SNS*, Chapter 5, "The God of this World," 85–113.

[73] Referred to as *SNS* or *Sacred, not Secret* (Melba: Worldwide United, 2008), written by Christopher, 85–113, https://www.realilluminati.org/sacred-not-secret.

[74] *SNS*, 49.

[75] Definition: "The part of your mind that controls your attitudes and behavior." *See* "psyche," in *Macmillan English Dictionary*, accessed March 29, 2020, https://www.macmillandictionary.com/us/dictionary/american/psyche.

(Eve), and the *Id* (Lucifer).[76] Therefore, our play presents *Lucifer* enticing *Eve* (vanity and pride enticing our ego).

Our play is very clear in its presentation that all religious prayers, of any degree of sincerity, are answered (by *Lucifer*) inside of a person's own head according to the person's beliefs, all of which are based on the person's vanity and pride.

Our 1842 play clearly presents the devil ("Lucifer, the god of this world"[77]) as the god of the LDS/Mormon people. Our play also presents the devil as the god of all other churches too, which are set up to get gain, to be popular in the eyes of the world, and to control the flesh (individual free will). Our play is clear that *Lucifer* is the ONLY god that hears and answers mortal prayers. As mentioned above, our play clearly shows that the characters that represent Heavenly Father (Elohim) and Jesus (Jehovah) are **not involved** with any mortal upon Earth. Furthermore, it

---

[76] Saul McLeod, "Id, ego and superego," *Simply psychology*, September 25, 2019, https://www.simplypsychology.org/psyche.html.

　See also Cynthia Vinney, "Freud: Id, Ego, and Superego Explained," *ThoughtCo.*, February 28, 2019, https://www.thoughtco.com/id-ego-and-superego-4582342.

[77] *SNS*, Chapter 5, 85–113.

shows that when a person prays, no matter how sincerely, only *Lucifer* is there to give revelation, inspiration, and answers to their prayers.

We have explained that this god (*Lucifer*) is nothing more or less than one's own human nature, which is responsible for their pride and ego. We wrote of this pride and tried to make it perfectly clear what our *true God's* "intent to do good" means:

> But behold, hearken ye unto me, and know that by the help of the all-powerful Creator of heaven and earth I can tell you concerning your thoughts, how that ye are beginning to labor in sin, which sin appeareth very abominable unto me, yea, and abominable unto God.

> Yea, it grieveth my soul and causeth me to shrink with shame before the presence of my Maker, that I must testify unto you concerning the wickedness of your hearts.

And also it grieveth me that I must use so much boldness of speech concerning you, before your wives and your children, many of whose feelings are exceedingly tender and chaste and delicate before God, which thing is pleasing unto God;

And it supposeth me that they have come up hither to hear the pleasing word of God, yea, the word which healeth the wounded soul.

Wherefore, it burdeneth my soul that I should be constrained, because of the strict commandment which I have received from God, to admonish you according to your crimes, to enlarge the wounds of those who are already wounded, instead of consoling and healing their wounds; and those who have not been wounded, instead of feasting upon the pleasing word of God have daggers placed to pierce their souls and wound their delicate minds.

But, notwithstanding the greatness of the task, I must do according to the strict commands of God, and tell you concerning your wickedness and abominations, in the presence of the pure in heart, and the broken heart, and under the glance of the piercing eye of the Almighty God.

Wherefore, I must tell you the truth according to the plainness of the word of God. ...

And now behold, my brethren, this is the word which I declare unto you, that many of you have begun to search for gold, and for silver, and for all manner of precious ores, in the which this land, which is a land of promise unto you and to your seed, doth abound most plentifully.

And the hand of providence hath smiled upon you most pleasingly, that you have obtained many riches; and because some of you have obtained more abundantly than that of your brethren ye are lifted up in the pride of your hearts, and wear stiff necks and high heads because of the costliness of your apparel, and persecute your brethren because ye suppose that ye are better than they.

And now, my brethren, do ye suppose that God justifieth you in this thing? Behold, I say unto you, Nay. But he condemneth you, and if ye persist in these things his judgments must speedily come unto you.

O that he would show you that he can pierce you, and with one glance of his eye he can smite you to the dust!

O that he would rid you from this iniquity and abomination. And, O that ye would listen unto the word of his commands, and let not this pride of your hearts destroy your souls!

Think of your brethren like unto yourselves, and be familiar with all and free with your substance, that they may be rich like unto you.

But before ye seek for riches, seek ye for the kingdom of God.

And after ye have obtained a hope in Christ ye shall obtain riches, if ye seek them; **and ye will seek them for the intent to do good—to clothe the naked, and to feed the hungry, and to liberate the captive, and administer relief to the sick and the afflicted**.

And now, my brethren, I have spoken unto you concerning pride [Lucifer]; and those of you which have afflicted your neighbor, and persecuted him because ye were proud in your hearts, of the things which God hath given you, what say ye of it?

Do ye not suppose that such things are abominable unto him who created all flesh? And the one being is as precious in his sight as the other. And all flesh is of the dust; and for the selfsame end hath he created them, that they should keep his commandments and glorify him forever.[78]

In our *Book of Mormon*, we presented the story of an angel of God explaining the development of the United States of America. We had this angel tell Nephi (one of our main characters) that he would see the rest of the history of the world, although he was not allowed to write anything beyond the establishment of the United States of America. We intended for our book of Revelation in the Bible to tell the rest of the story.[79]

---

[78] *BOM*, Jacob 2:5–21, emphasis added.
[79] *BOM*, 1 Nephi 14:18–28.

We wrote Revelation in allegory and symbolism, as we would also later write and present our 1842 play.[80] Revelation is clear about what will happen to the "kings" and "merchants"[81] of this world when the "one like unto the Son of man rides on a white horse with a sharp two-edged sword coming out of his mouth."[82] (More about this allegoric representation is explained in Part Three (titled "A New American Jesus") of this five-part series introducing *A New American Scripture*.

According to Revelation, no person on Earth who has supposedly lived in sin (according to religion) will suffer when Revelation's presentation of a symbolic *Christ* comes to Earth to fight the secret combination of politics (kings) and business (merchants). These "kings and merchants" are the only ones who will suffer.[83]

---

[80] *Sacred, not Secret*, https://www.realilluminati.org/sacred-not-secret.

[81] Revelation 18:3.

[82] *See* Revelation 18:1; 19:11–21.

[83] Christopher, *666, The Mark of America—Seat of the Beast: The Apostle John's New Testament Revelation Unfolded* (Worldwide United, 2006), 395–6, https://www.realilluminati.org/666-mark-of-america. (Hereafter referred to as *666 America*.)

We patterned our Revelation's *Christ* character after the "Son of man"[84] that was presented in preceding New Testament stories. The parable written about the "Son of man" appearing in his glory to judge the world is clear about who will be condemned and who will be saved. According to Matthew, chapter 25, those who do *no* good to "the least of these"[85] are those who were presented on the "left hand"[86] of the Son of man when he comes in his glory. Those whose intent was to do good to "the least of these"[87] are judged and placed on his right hand.[88]

This final judgment (presented in Matthew's parable and referred to in Revelation), is given by the "Son of man," who comes in his glory to judge the nations of Earth. This "judgment" is solely based on whether or not a person lived their life with "the intent to do good—to clothe the naked, and to feed the hungry, and to liberate the captive,

---

[84] Matthew 16:13; 25:31.
[85] Matthew 25:45.
[86] Matthew 25:41.
[87] Matthew 25:40.
[88] Matthew 25:31–46.

and administer relief to the sick and the afflicted."[89] The final judgment of humanity[90] is based on this alone. **Nothing more. Nothing less.**

According to these scriptures, it is very clear that the only ones who will suffer an "everlasting punishment"[91] are those people who did *not* "seek for riches ... for the intent to do good."[92] (In other words, they sought for riches for other reasons or intents, i.e. worldly success and popularity, costly apparel,[93] churches, temples, malls,[94] etc.)

Our new American scripture presents this blatant hypocrisy of the churches that claim to follow Christ ("the Son of man"). Instead of dedicating their religion's doctrines, principles, and commandments "for the intent to

---

[89] *BOM*, Jacob 2:19.

[90] "We will judge ourselves." in Anonymous, *Human Reality—Who We Are and Why We Exist!* (Melba: Worldwide United, 2009), 517.

[91] Matthew 25:46.

[92] *See BOM*, Jacob 2:19; Matthew 25:31–46.

[93] *BOM*, Alma 4:6.

[94] Alice Hines, "City Creek, Mormon Shopping Mall, Boasts Flame-Shooting Fountains, Biblical Splendor (Photos)," *HuffPost*, March 22, 2012, https://www.huffpost.com/entry/city-creek-mormon-mall_n_1372695.

do good,"[95] Christian churches seek for riches "to get gain, to get power over the flesh, to become popular in the eyes of the world, and seek the lusts of the flesh and the things of the world."[96] And no modern Christian church has been more successful at ignoring the basic principles of Jesus' teachings and warnings than the church that evolved from claiming belief in our *Book of Mormon*—the Church of Jesus Christ of Latter-day Saints.

The *intent* for which this mainstream Mormon religion uses our writings as scripture manifests itself in what it has become. This religion is one of the (if not the) wealthiest religions on Earth.[97] This church "gets gain" from its tithing and donations, from its investments and economic strategies.[98]

We ask those who read our new American scripture,

---

[95] *BOM*, Jacob 2:19.

[96] *BOM*, 1 Nephi 22:23.

[97] "List of wealthiest organizations," *Wikipedia, The Free Encyclopedia*, last modified March 20, 2020, https://en.wikipedia.org/wiki/List_of_wealthiest_organizations#Religious_organizations.

[98] Paul Glader, "Mormon Church Stockpiled $100 Billion Intended for Charities and Misled LDS Members, Whistleblower Says," *Newsweek* and *Religion Unplugged*, December 17, 2019, https://www.newsweek.com/mormon-church-stockpiled-100-billion-intended-charities-misled-lds-members-whistleblower-says-1477809.

<u>Why have ye built up churches unto yourselves to get gain?[99]</u>

Although the idea of tithing is seldom mentioned in the *Book of Mormon*, it *is* addressed according to the words of Malachi (which we also wrote for the Bible). In our new America scripture, we presented how the King James Bible had been transfigured and had many of its "plain and precious parts" removed.[100] Upon the commencement of our work, publishing *The Sealed Portion* [of the *Book of Mormon*]—*The Final Testament of Jesus Christ,* we also put the "plain and precious parts" back into the corrupted version of the King James book of Malachi.[101]

When the correct translation from the original Greek words of Malachi is read, Christian ecclesiastical priesthood authority is greatly condemned for its misuse of

---

[99] *BOM*, Mormon 8:32–3.
[100] *BOM*, 1 Nephi 13:26–9.
[101] *See* "The Book of Malachi," *Real Illuminati*™, accessed March 29, 2020, https://www.realilluminati.org/the-book-of-malachi.

tithing. The original words of Malachi present tithing for the sake of the poor and needy … for the intent to do good.

The LDS/Mormon Church attempts to defend itself by claiming and touting its millions of dollars in humanitarian aid, goods, and services given to poor regions of the world. This church pays no attention to the negative effect that its humanitarian efforts have on these poor communities and cultures. Instead of helping these people, the Mormons contribute to and perpetuate the destruction of the ability of the local people to develop a sustainable economic infrastructure for themselves.[102] We have proven this unchallengeable fact through a *Memorandum* we published that thoroughly counters that Church's fraudulent charitable claims.[103] There is no doubt that Mormon humanitarian efforts, as well as most other

---

[102] "In every area of the world where poverty existed before the LDS Church began its humanitarian efforts, the local economy was left devastated, and much worse off than it was before LDS efforts began," *in* "Memorandum," *The Humanity Party® Board of Directors in collaboration with The Marvelous Work and a Wonder®*, accessed March 29, 2020, https://humanityparty.com/press_conference/05_28_18/Memorandum.pdf.
[103] "Memorandum."

humanitarian/charitable efforts, destroy local economic infrastructures and exacerbate poverty.

In our new scripture, we implored the American Christians to "believe in Christ,"[104] to believe in his words, to believe in "his judgments."[105] These judgments couldn't be more clearly outlined than they are in the twenty-fifth chapter of Matthew,[106] and further in the book of Revelation.[107]

We warned the Gentiles, "seeing that ye know the light by which ye may judge, which is the light of Christ,[108] see that ye do not judge wrongfully."[109]

The goal and intent of our new American scripture was to influence early American European Christians to do good—not "good" according to the "god of this world"[110] (who hears and answers their prayers and gives their religious leaders revelation and inspiration), but "good"

---

[104] *BOM*, 2 Nephi 25:16.

[105] *See BOM*, 2 Nephi 25:16–30; 33:10.

[106] Matthew 25:31–46; *see also* Matthew 7:21–7.

[107] Revelation 18:5–24; *see also 666 America*, 325–30, 423–6.

[108] *BOM*, Moroni 7:18–19.

[109] *See BOM*, Moroni 7:18.

[110] *BOM*, Moroni 7:14; *SNS*, Chapter 5, 85–113.

according to the *true Christ and God* that *fights* the pride of the god of this world.[111]

This true Christ and God is the *true* "Spirit of Christ"[112] given to every person upon Earth equally. It is our unique human common sense. It is our human conscience that allows us to "know good from evil," and shows us "the way to judge" between something that is good and something that is evil.[113]

As we wrote our new scripture intended for early European American Christians, we counseled Joseph Smith to allow some of his peers to preview our new scripture. After 116 pages of handwritten manuscript were complete, Joseph was instructed to show it to a selected few people, which included some who were very critical of Joseph's claims. This initial peer review group was disturbed by how we intended to present all religion, all ordinance, all ritual, and all priesthood as "evil." None could let go of their

---

[111] *BOM*, Moroni 7:14; *SNS*, Chapter 5, 85–113.
[112] *BOM*, Moroni 7:16–17.
[113] *BOM*, Moroni 7:15–16.

religious feelings enough to accept that <u>ALL</u> religion was corrupt and unneeded for the salvation of humanity.

Accordingly, in order to get early American Christians to consider reading our new scripture, we had to change the story so that it did not include a clear condemnation of all religion, of every kind and manner. Nevertheless, we inserted many clues about this Real Truth throughout our rewrite of the storyline.

We wanted to clearly and unmistakably address the religions that we knew were corrupt. Knowing that it was very possible that the people who first followed Joseph Smith would corrupt the intent of our book, we included a prophecy directed specifically at them:

> Behold, I speak unto you as if ye were present, and yet ye are not. But behold, Jesus Christ hath shown you unto me, and I know your doing.[114]

We then made it perfectly clear what their "doing" is:

---

[114] *BOM*, Mormon 8:35.

And I know that ye do walk in the pride of your hearts; and there are none save a few only who do not lift themselves up in the pride of their hearts, unto the wearing of very fine apparel, unto envying, and strifes, and malice, and persecutions, and all manner of iniquities; and your churches, yea, even every one, have become polluted because of the pride of your hearts.

For behold, ye do love money, and your substance, and your fine apparel, and the adorning of your churches, more than ye love the poor and the needy, the sick and the afflicted.

O ye pollutions, ye hypocrites, ye teachers, who sell yourselves for that which will canker, why have ye polluted the holy church of God? Why are ye ashamed to take upon you the name of Christ? Why do ye not think that greater is the value of an endless happiness than that misery which never dies—<u>because of the praise of the world?</u>

Why do ye adorn yourselves with that which hath no life, and yet suffer the hungry, and the needy, and the naked, and the sick and the afflicted to pass by you, and notice them not?

Yea, why do ye build up your secret abominations to get gain, and cause that widows should mourn before the Lord, and also orphans to mourn before the Lord, and also the blood of their fathers and their husbands to cry unto the Lord from the ground, for vengeance upon your heads?

Behold, the sword of vengeance hangeth over you; and the time soon cometh that he avengeth the blood of the saints upon you, for he will not suffer their cries any longer.[115]

---

[115] *See BOM*, Mormon 8:36–41.

Latter-day Saint Mormons are very deceptive to the rest of the world through their missionary efforts. People are attracted to Mormon missionaries because of the hope that the United States of America presents to the rest of the world ... the *American Dream*.[116]

Although they ignore every doctrine, principle, and message of our book, Mormons use it to entice people to join *their* church. Our book is this religion's main selling point. Mormons call it the "keystone of our religion."[117] The early Mormon Church made many different attempts to recruit new members. These efforts included ships filled with European-Mormon converts headed for America with the promise of God's support and blessing in building up the *Mormon* "Kingdom of God."[118] Mormon missionaries are sent throughout the world today to seduce poor people into joining their religion. They do this by asking people to

---

[116] *666 America*, 295.

[117] *BOM*, "Introduction," which Introduction was *not* in the original *BOM*, but was added by the LDS/Mormons in 1981.

[118] *D&C*, 65:2. *See also* Bruce D. Porter, "Building the Kingdom," *The Church of Jesus Christ of Latter-day Saints*, April 1, 2001, https://www.churchofjesuschrist.org/study/general-conference/2001/04/building-the-kingdom.

read our book[119] (the *Book of Mormon*). Our book presents America as God's new "promised land," filled with opportunity and protected by the "power of God."[120]

The poor have a vision and perception of America. America is known as the land of opportunity and wealth. When an American missionary shows up on the doorstep of a poor family's home, the family is very interested in, first, why they were privileged to be picked to have Americans speak to them, and secondly, how America became as great as it is.

But the Mormon hook is what catches the poor off guard and reels them in: "If you join our Church, you can be with your family forever."[121] This is the Mormons' greatest modern selling point, a point and doctrine that is diametrically and unequivocally opposed to the "fullness

---

[119] "The Book of Mormon, 1830 Edition," *Real Illuminati™*, accessed March 29, 2020, https://www.realilluminati.org/the-book-of-mormon.

[120] *BOM*, 1 Nephi 13:13–19.

[121] Henry B. Eyring, "Families Can Be Together Forever," *Church of Jesus Christ of Latter-day Saints*, June 2015, https://www.churchofjesuschrist.org/study/ensign/2015/06/families-can-be-together-forever.

"The Plan of Salvation," *The Church of Jesus Christ of Latter-day Saints*, March 29, 2020, https://www.churchofjesuschrist.org/study/manual/preach-my-gospel-a-guide-to-missionary-service/lesson-2-the-plan-of-salvation.

of the everlasting Gospel ... as delivered by the Savior,"[122] as presented in our new American scripture.

Poor people envy the lifestyles that these missionaries seem to have. As an investigator reads our book, they discover why and how God made the United States of America the greatest nation on Earth, "above all other nations."[123] The investigator is convinced that our book is true because of the perception that the United States *is* the greatest nation on Earth, and that the image of the *American Dream*[124] is worth considering.

It's obvious to the rest of the world that the United States has the most powerful military. It's obvious that the United States is the most powerful economic force in the world. So, when two well-dressed Americans show up at a poor person's door with a message from God, it is easy to convince non-American Christians that there must be something that God has done to make America what it is. Maybe these two Mormon missionaries can explain how

---

[122] *PGP, JSH* 1:34.
[123] *BOM*, 1 Nephi 13:30.
[124] *666 America*, 295.

the United States became what it is ... at least that is for what the hopeless living in a third world country in abject poverty hope.

Reading our book about how God has been behind America and made it what it is manipulates the reader to assume that the religion that is represented by the missionaries *might* be the only true and living church of God on Earth.[125]

With the implied promise of a better life, the poor of this world have been deceived into joining that Church. However, the deception of a new hope and life by becoming Mormon, as well as being sealed as an eternal family unit, are not the tools that are used to convert the heart and soul of the investigator; OUR BOOK IS!

We wrote the *Book of Mormon* in a way that we knew would touch the spiritual underpinnings and religious hopes and susceptibilities of a normal human. From years of experience, we knew what we needed to write in order to create a spiritual, special feeling "inside the bosom"[126]

---

[125] Oaks, "The Only True and Living Church."
[126] *D&C*, 9:8–9.

as one reads our words. Upon reading our book with a sincere heart and real intent, a person is left with *spiritual* evidence that our book *must be* from God.

Mormon missionaries use the spiritual feelings that people get from reading our book to deceive an investigator into believing that the Mormon Church is the only true church of God on Earth. Once spiritually convinced, the unsuspecting investigator is presented with a bait and switch. Deceived by the spiritual feelings one gets while reading our book, the unsuspecting investigator is snared in a trap, believing that "If the *Book of Mormon* is true, then the Mormon Church must be true."

The bait and switch works almost every time!

After joining the Church, it is no longer a requirement to pay attention to the *Book of Mormon*. But it <u>is</u> a requirement to listen to and obey the Church leaders. And if one wants to have an eternal family unit, they must pay a FULL tithe to the Church (10% of their income).[127]

---

[127] "The Law of Tithing," in *Teachings of Presidents of the Church: Howard W. Hunter* (Salt Lake City: The Church of Jesus Christ of Latter-day Saints, 2015), 133, accessed March 29, 2020,

The "fulness of the everlasting Gospel … as delivered by the Savior to the [ancient native Americans]"[128] is subtly replaced with vain oblations, temple rituals and other priesthood ordinances, and many prayers … just as Isaiah states had happened to the church of God in ancient times among the Hebrews.[129]

The world sleeps in ignorance. The world has "closed your eyes, and the prophets and your rulers, the seers are covered. And the vision of all is become unto you as the words of a book that is sealed"[130] that no one can read or understand. While this has all been going on, a secret combination of religious, political, and business powers has become one of the WEALTHIEST INSTITUTIONS IN THE ENTIRE WORLD![131]

No institution can become this wealthy if its purpose is to establish something of worth to humanity, in which the poor can trust.

---

https://www.churchofjesuschrist.org/study/manual/teachings-of-presidents-of-the-church-howard-w-hunter/chapter-9-the-law-of-tithing.

[128] *PGP*, JSH 1:34.

[129] *See* Isaiah, chapter 1.

[130] *Compare* Isaiah 29:10–11; *see also BOM*, 2 Nephi 27:10.

[131] *Wikipedia*, "List of wealthiest organizations."

The Church of Jesus Christ of Latter-day Saints (LDS/Mormon Church) outlines thirteen (13) of its Articles of Faith. One article specifically announces

the literal gathering of Israel and ... the restoration of the Ten Tribes; that Zion (the New Jerusalem) will be built upon the American continent; that Christ will reign personally upon the earth; and, that the earth will be renewed and receive its paradisiacal glory.[132]

We have named this particular Church the most evil institution that has ever existed on Earth.[133] We consider it to be the "most evil" because it has been given the most information and the greatest chance and opportunity to do the right thing.

In our *Book of Mormon*, we outlined *what* the right thing that a "pure religion, undefiled before God"[134] should

---

[132] *PGP*, The Articles of Faith, 10.

[133] "Wherefore, take heed, my beloved brethren, that ye do not judge that which is evil to be of God, or that which is good and of God to be of the devil. (*BOM*, Moroni 7:14.)

[134] James 1:27.

do. In our outline, we took nothing away from the Christian Bible, but added information that was consistent with European-American Christian beliefs.

Instead of incorporating the "fulness of the everlasting gospel … as delivered by the Savior to the ancient inhabitants"[135] living on the American continent, this evil institution has done the exact opposite. When given opportunity and free agency, the Church of Jesus Christ of Latter-day Saints (Mormon Church) has proven what people choose when they follow *Lucifer* (their pride and ego)—*the god of this world*.[136]

The Church should be paying attention to the great words of Isaiah about the *uselessness* of religious ordinances, meetings, and other religious-based rituals.[137] It should "learn to do well; seek judgment, relieve the oppressed, judge the fatherless, plead for the widow."[138] Instead, the Mormon Church fills its members' time with useless rituals and ordinances, vain and baseless

---

[135] *PGP*, JSH 1:34.

[136] *SNS*, Chapter 5, 85–113.

[137] *See* Isaiah, Chapter 1.

[138] Isaiah 1:16–17.

genealogies, temple attendance, and everything else that Isaiah spoke against.

The contemporary *Mormon gospel* has nothing to do with what our *Book of Mormon* Jesus told the ancient American people, as we presented it in our book. If asked what the "fulness of the everlasting gospel of Christ"[139] is, the typical Mormon response is everything *except* that which our Jesus taught the people.

In our book, *The True History of Religion*, we explained why and how we tried to use religion to help set up an organization that could help humanity, especially in distributing the basic necessities of life to all of Earth's inhabitants. Instead of our efforts through religion leading to this end, our book (the *Book of Mormon*) was hijacked and helped create one of the wealthiest religious organizations in modern history.[140]

There were other time periods when humanity flourished and were much more advanced than humans

---

[139] *PGP*, JSH 1:34.

[140] "5 Richest Religious Organizations In The World," *2 Minute Facts*, accessed April 3, 2020, https://2minutefacts.com/5-richest-religious-organizations-in-the-world/.

are today.[141] However, there was no time during Earth's past, in any other time period, where there existed a belief-based organization with the amount of money and influence of the secret combination of religion, politics, and business that has developed as the Church of Jesus Christ of Latter-day Saints.

We did not reveal the Real Truth (true identity) of our *allegoric Jesus Christ*[142] until *after* we had done <u>everything possible</u> to infiltrate the hard hearts and closed minds of the members of this wealthy religious organization. We had hoped that it could help us end worldwide poverty.[143] The Mormon Church has the infrastructure, money, and means that could have helped us launch many of the solutions to humanity's problems.[144] We instructed our current True Messenger to offer our assistance to help the LDS/Mormon

---

[141] *See THOR*, Chapter 1.

[142] Given by Christopher on December 20, 2016 via Facebook Live video.

[143] "The Humanity Party®'s Plan to Eliminate Worldwide Poverty Explained!" The Humanity Party®, September 17, 2016, https://www.youtube.com/watch?v=kQ_Rlm_pC_k.

[144] Peggy Fletcher Stack, "LDS Church kept the lid on its $100B fund for fear tithing receipts would fall, account boss tells Wall Street Journal," *The Salt Lake Tribune*, February 8, 2020, https://www.sltrib.com/news/2020/02/08/lds-church-kept-lid-its-b/.

Church to do the right thing. This church ignored us and rejected our existence.[145]

Our book has become obsolete to the Mormons. Our book has no part of the Mormon "gospel of Jesus Christ"[146] as presented to the world by the Church of Jesus Christ of Latter-day Saints. The leaders of this religion use our book for their own purposes, instead of for the reasons for which we wrote it.

The machinations of these purveyors of injustice must be stopped and their deception and fraud finally exposed. These are the reasons why we are writing *A New American Scripture—How and Why the Real Illuminati™ Created the Book of Mormon*.

The intent of that book will be to take back the power of our work[147] by explaining how and why our *Book of Mormon* was created. It will give exact details of how this

---

[145] Christopher, "Letter to The First Presidency," 596–7.

[146] M. Russell Ballard, "The True, Pure, and Simple Gospel of Jesus Christ," *The Church of Jesus Christ of Latter-day Saints*, April 6, 2019, https://www.churchofjesuschrist.org/study/general-conference/2019/04/23ballard.

[147] "One Race, One People, One World—The Humanity Party®," *Real Illuminati™*, 2019, https://www.realilluminati.org.

evil religious institution has violated "the fulness of the everlasting gospel ... as delivered by the Savior to the ancient inhabitants of the American continent."[148]

It is wrong, it is evil, to amass billions of dollars in savings. It is wrong to build a multibillion-dollar mall (City Creek Mall)[149] that entices people to become members of the "great and abominable church of the devil."[150] It is wrong to put yourself above any other human on Earth. It is wrong to use our scripture to convert people and then preach a gospel that has nothing to do with the "fullness of the everlasting Gospel delivered by the Savior."[151]

It is wrong to do anything except that for which a "hope in Christ"[152] should inspire a person. A proper understanding and hope of Christ will inspire a person **to do good—to clothe the naked, and to feed the hungry, and to liberate the captive, and administer relief to the sick and the afflicted.**"[153]

---

[148] *See PGP*, JSH 1:34.

[149] "City Creek Center," *Wikipedia, The Free Encyclopedia*, last modified January 8, 2020, https://en.wikipedia.org/wiki/City_Creek_Center.

[150] *See BOM*, 1 Nephi, chapters 13–14.

[151] *PGP*, JSH 1:34.

[152] *BOM*, Jacob 2:19.

[153] *BOM*, Jacob 2:19, emphasis added.

There should be no other purpose for "pure religion, undefiled before God," but "to visit the fatherless and widows in their affliction, and to keep himself unspotted from the world."[154]

Isaiah of the Old Testament says it. The New Testament Jesus and his disciples say it. And our new American scripture drives this point home.

This will always be our intent: to do good.

---

[154] James 1:27.

Above All Other Nations

Part Two

Few humans on Earth are as proud of their nation as Americans are. Americans are vain in their belief that just because they are citizens of the United States they are better than everyone else in the world.

As we presented in our 1842 play, and explained in Part One of this book, *Lucifer* (one's pride and ego responsible for human nature), *the God of this world*,[155] is responsible for the current state of the United States of America.

Americans could have used, and still can use, the power of their nation to do good for the rest of the world. Instead, their pride and vanity have created what they believe is the greatest nation on Earth, above all other nations.[156] They secure their borders with their power and

---

[155] *SNS*, Chapter 5, 85–113.
[156] *BOM*, 1 Nephi 13:30.

arrogance,[157] all of which is given to them by *their pride and ego, the God of the American people.*

This pride and vanity has resulted in modern Americans consuming more antidepressant drugs than the people of any other nation on Earth.[158]

Why?

Because the "hardness of their hearts and the blindness of their minds [has] brought [them] down into captivity, and also into destruction, both temporally and spiritually."[159] This is exactly how drugs *captivate* the unsuspecting user and cause an addiction that destroys them, both temporally and spiritually.

Ironically, of all of the religions in the entire world, the members of the Church of Jesus Christ of Latter-day

---

[157] "Border Security," *Department of Homeland Security*, last modified February 25, 2019, https://www.dhs.gov/topic/border-security.

[158] E.J. Mundell, "Antidepressant use in U.S. soars by 65 percent in 15 years," *CBS News*, August 16, 2017, https://www.cbsnews.com/news/antidepressant-use-soars-65-percent-in-15-years/;

Maggie Fox, "One in 6 Americans Take Antidepressants, Other Psychiatric Drugs: Study," *NBC News*, December 12, 2016, https://www.nbcnews.com/health/health-news/one-6-americans-take-antidepressants-other-psychiatric-drugs-n695141;

Skye Gould and Lauren F Friedman, "Something startling is going on with antidepressant use around the world," *Business Insider*, February 4, 2016, https://www.businessinsider.com/countries-largest-antidepressant-drug-users-2016-2.

[159] *BOM*, 1 Nephi 14:7.

Saints take more prescription drugs for depression (per capita) than any other people of any other religious group ON EARTH![160]

We warned Americans what would happen if they rejected the message of our new American scripture:

For the time cometh, saith the Lamb of God, that I will work a great and a marvelous work among the children of men; a work which shall be everlasting, either on the one hand or on the other—either to the convincing of them unto peace and life eternal, or unto the deliverance of them to the hardness of their hearts and the blindness of their minds unto their being brought down into captivity, and also into destruction, both temporally and spiritually, according to the captivity of the devil, of which I have spoken.[161]

---

[160] Julie Cart, "Study Finds Utah Leads Nation in Antidepressant Use, *LA Times*, February 20, 2002, https://www.latimes.com/archives/la-xpm-2002-feb-20-mn-28924-story.html;
   See also Russell Goldman, "Two Studies Find Depression Widespread in Utah," *ABC News*, February 9, 2009, https://abcnews.go.com/Health/MindMoodNews/story?id=4403731&page=1.
[161] *BOM*, 1 Nephi 14:7.

Our work, a Marvelous Work and a Wonder®, can help humanity establish peace on Earth. Our work can convince a person of "life eternal" by explaining the Real Truth about human existence—who we are and why we exist.

We intentionally wrote that our work can "convinc[e] them <u>unto</u> peace and life eternal,"[162] because our work teaches that each person is an equal life form of the highest capacity and capability. There are no other life forms, anywhere in the universe or in any other dimension, greater than the human form.

Our work teaches, and has the power to convince, that life experience on Earth is *not* who we *really* are— that mortal existence is similar to a *dream experience* that our mortal minds create subconsciously while dreaming. Mortal life seems more real, structured, and purposed than what mortals perceive as their sleeping dreams. This is because the Earth experience of Mortal Life occurs in the subconsciousness of the highly

---

[162] 1 Nephi 14:7.

advanced brain of our True Self[163] (which is of the highest form and capability).

No matter how clearly we try to explain it, no matter how much logical and empirical evidence we try to provide, a normal mortal mind finds it difficult to fully comprehend and accept the reality of our eternal human nature. Mortals were never *supposed* to comprehend this, any more than your *dream Self* comprehends that the experiences you have while dreaming are only a dream.

One does not realize that a dream is "just a dream" until that person wakes up. After mortal death, *awakened* in our true reality as highly advanced human beings, all people will realize that their mortal life was no more significant to their *true reality* than a mortal dream is to their daily human reality on Earth.

Our work can lead a person *unto* the realization that each person is actually experiencing *life eternal.* Again, this Real Truth will become self-evident once the mortal brain loses the connectivity it has with one's True Self

---

[163] *See THOR* (large print), 1–31 for further study.

upon experiencing a mortal death.[164] (The True Self will continue to exist. We present this concept in our 1842 play,[165] through clear and convincing allegoric parts and scenes. The *god Michael* is put to sleep and *dreams* that he is the *mortal Adam*.)[166]

In the near future, the processes and procedures of science will provide substantial proof of the probability that human life upon Earth is nothing more or less than an experience occurring in the subconscious mind of a highly advanced brain. For example, virtual experiences generated by preprogrammed computer software will allow a mortal person to connect to a game with a brain-to-computer connection. The computer's software will then send electrical impulses into the brain that cause the *player* to see, smell, hear, taste, and feel things that are not part of the player's *real* world, but rather are generated by the computer's stimulation. At any time, the player can stop the game and disconnect.

---

[164] *THOR* (large print), 22.

[165] *Sacred, not Secret*, https://www.realilluminati.org/sacred-not-secret.

[166] *SNS*, 35–6, 49.

This disconnection procedure will be as simple as taking off a headset, or, with more advanced technology, sending a voluntary brain impulse (a thought sent wirelessly) instructing the game to pause or end. This loss of connectivity (in the same way as mortal death is currently pronounced when one is "brain dead") will return the player to their *real, true reality*.

The reality of experiencing a virtual reality that is not *really* part of the life experience on Earth, except as it occurs and is restricted inside of the brain, will become a Real Truth as soon as science and technology advances sufficiently. When many are able to experience this advanced *game playing*, then the idea that our Earth experience is voluntarily created in the brain of a highly advanced life form (human) will be much easier for people to accept.

We support science because we understand science. Science is the way that humans attempt to solve life's mysteries. In reality, there is no mystery to life. There is only ignorance of what life is and how it is. We have done everything within our power to influence the progress and innovation of science ... always for the intent to do good.

One of the reasons why humans living on Earth do not know who they *really* are, is because their mortal brain is constructed so that they cannot know this for sure. Not even the strictest scientific minds can ignore that people often *feel* some sort of connection outside of their mortal self. At least the *feeling* appears to come from something extrinsic (outside of one's own mind). A person can play a computer game with such intensity and purpose that their *real* world disappears, until they choose to end the experience and make a choice to return their focus and concentration to mortal reality.

There is no power on Earth or anywhere else in the vast universe that can keep an individual from committing suicide ... NONE. This fact alone proves the power of the individual in controlling their own destiny and their own reality. No god, no dictator, no one outside of one's own self can stop one from ending one's life, if one desires to end it.

Therefore, there should be no argument about the free will of the individual and the power and control that each has equally.

This individual power is free will. Nothing is more important to human reality and human nature than the ability of a person to do what that person *wants* to do. Free will is what makes humans different from all other animals. Humans seek their own individual personal happiness. If this search is impeded by something, then this "something" irritates the person, causing the opposite of peace (which is strife and conflict).

When considered correctly and honestly, <u>all</u> strife and conflict occur when a person is unable to do what the person wants in the pursuit of individual happiness. So, in order for the Earth experience to provide a person with success at finding happiness, nothing can exist that impedes human free will.

Some argue that people cannot be allowed to exercise unconditional free will because the unimpeded exercising thereof might hinder the free will of another. This is true and is the purpose for the right laws and the right form of government.[167]

We have introduced three main principles for the right form of human government, all of which support and protect individual free will:

First Principle

Government Exists For The Benefit of the People Only

The First Principle is that this government shall never be self-serving; or in other words, it shall never act in and of itself and of its own accord for the sake of its own existence.

---

[167] "HOPE For America's Future," *The Humanity Party*® (*THumP*®), 2017, https://www.humanityparty.com.

Second Principle

Government Exists To Protect Individual Free Will

The Second Principle is that this government will guarantee the freedom, or the free agency, of all those whom it serves.

Third Principle

Government Exists To Support and Protect Life

The Third Principle of government is that it shall provide the means whereby those whom it serves may have an equal opportunity to experience the happiness each person desires, as long as that desire is consistent with the Second Principle of government regarding personal free agency.[168]

The only laws that should be enacted are those that conform with these three principles.

---

[168] "One Race, One People, One World," https://www.realilluminati.org.

For example, if a person is happy listening to loud music, then the person should be protected and supported in listening to loud music, as long as doing so does not expose another to the loud music who is not happy listening to it. Playing music too loud should be prohibited by law, but only as long as the person who desires to listen to loud music is still able to. Without science and technology, this type of law would not be possible, nor fair for all equally. Modern headphones provide a way that a law prohibiting the public playing of loud music can be the right law for all. Without headphones that isolate the loud music to the individual, this law would not fulfill the Second Principle (above) of the right form of government.[169]

Using the above simple analogy of a type of law that protects one person from not being forced to comply with another person's free will to listen to loud music, how should the one who invents the headphones be rewarded for inventing them?

---

[169] "The Constitution of The United People of the Republic of America," *The Humanity Party*®, accessed March 29, 2020, https://humanityparty.com/proposed-constitution.

This is where the value of money and free market policies come into play (the right form of Capitalism).[170] If there's a law that prohibits a person from playing loud music in public, and someone creates a way for a person to play their loud music whenever the person wants to and can still abide by the law, then the person who invents the headphones should be properly rewarded for supporting righteous laws of free will.

In this way, a few among the many have become extremely wealthy. The few have provided things that the many want in order to better exercise individual free will. Therefore, how can these few be blamed or punished for providing a way so that others can exercise their free will?

The third book of our Trilogy: *One People, One World, One Government*[171] will explain in detail how the right form of Capitalism can be established (by law). This

---

[170] "The Humanity Party® Political Platform," *The Humanity Party®*, 2017, https://humanityparty.com/thump-platform.

    See also "The Cause and Effect of Capitalism and Socialism on Humanity," *The Humanity Party®*, February 11, 2018, https://voicehumanity.tumblr.com/post/170751913294/the-battle-for-venezuela.

[171] The Real Illuminati™, *One People, One World, One Government*, (Melba: Worldwide United, upcoming), https://www.realilluminati.org/one-people-one-world-one-goverment.

form of government will support the free will[172] of one person to become wealthy by providing those things that everyone else wants to have in order to pursue individual free will and happiness.

Laws should exist, not to punish a person's free will to pursue wealth by providing the *wants* of humanity, but to protect everyone else's free will from being affected by that person's desire (free will) to become wealthy.

Again, consider our above hypothetical using headphones as an example. How is humanity hurt by a person inventing something that others *want*, especially those things that support individual free will?

One would assume that providing headphones so that people can play their music as loud as they want, whenever and wherever they want, would be a great benefit to humanity. But how are the headphones made? Of what are the headphones made? What happened to the earth's environment when the headphones were made?

---

[172] *See* "What is the purpose of the Real Illuminati™?" *under* "Frequently Asked Questions," *Real Illuminati™*, accessed April 4, 2020, https://www.realilluminati.org/faq-s; *see also THOR* (large print), 39–40.

What happened to the earth when the materials needed to create the headphones were extracted from Earth's natural environs?

Headphones need magnets. The iron ore magnetite has to be extracted from the environment. What does this extraction and manufacturing process do to the environment that is shared by all people equally?

The right form of government will enact laws that allow a person to become as wealthy as one desires (by providing the *wants* of other free-willed people), as long as in providing these wants the one does not destroy the environment or impede the free will of all others.

Is this possible? Yes.

How?

The following is a Real Truth about human life upon Earth that is not accepted by science and especially not by religion, but it is the Real Truth that we hope humans will one day be able to accept:

Using our example above, there were a few ancient civilizations[173] that had the correct form of government set up. The technology and science of these civilizations were far more advanced than those of today (2020).

Again, hypothetically, there was a law that prohibited the loud playing of music. Someone had the idea to create headphones. They needed magnets. The laws of the correct government prohibited these inventors from digging up a lot of earth to get the iron ore magnetite. Earth's environment was shared by others who didn't want to see the results of mining operations.

The solution was simple: create a planet in space, away from Earth, where magnetite could be extracted without impeding anyone's free will. These ancient highly advanced scientists figured out how to create a new planet (Mars, for example). This new planet had the necessary materials for some people to invent those things that other people wanted on Earth.

---

[173] *THOR* (large print), 39

Mining on Mars didn't pollute Earth or disrupt the natural environment on Earth enjoyed by others, who didn't particularly like listening to loud music. In this hypothetical, Mars produced all of the minerals and materials that any inventor needed to fulfill the *wants* of the masses, without causing any destruction to Earth's environs.

But what about the actual *needs* of the masses? The earth does not naturally create headphones. But Earth *does* naturally produce the things that its inhabitants *need* in order to live.

The greatest mistake of all human governments is in the absence of laws that protect, support, and guarantee the things that all of Earth's inhabitants *need* in order to live. Before one can exercise free will (possibly inventing headphones and becoming wealthy), one must be able to live. One cannot concentrate on inventing something that others *want*, and in supplying this *want* become wealthy, unless one has the free will and time to invent it. The first, foremost, and most important priority of the correct form of government is to guarantee that each person has what each *needs* in order to live.

The earth always provided the things that people *needed* in order to live, in the beginning, free of charge to its inhabitants. But when certain groups take control of the earth and its natural resources, they take away the free will of everyone else to have the things that they *need* in order to live. The masses are controlled by the few groups who control the natural resources of Earth, each group with its own form of government.

We know what is presented above, because we (the Real Illuminati™) know the Real Truth about human history. We have evidence that there were once great civilizations that were destroyed from within because of the inability of humans to establish and support the right form of government that serves all people equally. Once destroyed, pockets of survivors remained; but they did not retain the knowledge to re-form these great civilizations.

To make a long history of events short, the discovery and establishment of the United States of America was an attempt to set up the right form of government ... "above all other nations."[174]

Our work can convince a person "unto peace"[175] by explaining the Real Truth about human existence, and more importantly, presenting solutions that protect and support free will. This is the intent of our work—it always has been and it always will be. This was our intent in being involved with the establishment of the United States of America.

In the first book of our Trilogy, *The True History of Religion*, we explained that we search the world for the right cultures that are progressing towards a better world.[176] We determine if a culture is properly progressing based on what we know needs to happen in order for the right changes to be possible. We rely on our cumulative experience, each of us having different personal experience in many parts of the world where we have lived.

---

[174] *BOM*, 1 Nephi 13:30.
[175] *BOM*, 1 Nephi 14:7.
[176] *THOR* (large print), 48.

We search among the world's cultures for individuals who seem to have the most influence for change, but more importantly, the *desire* for change.[177]

This searching brought two of our group to South America as Spain and Portugal were developing new colonies in the 16th century CE. We found that neither of these two European Christian nations were establishing a presence in the Western Hemisphere for the good of the people, both immigrant and native. Our experience of living among these early South American developing colonies convinced us that we would have no influence there. We turned our attention further north to the developing colonies of America.

The American people of the United States do not realize that their nation was founded, not on democracy or the values or rights associated with the least among them, but on a secret combination of political, business, and religious powers.[178]

---

[177] Two examples of people we approached were Thomas Jefferson and Ethan Smith. *See THOR*, 183–8, 289, 195.

[178] *THOR* (large print), xxvi–xxx ("Introduction," 26–30).

One of our contemporary friends, Howard Zinn,[179] wrote of Christopher Columbus'[180] first encounter with the Western Hemisphere's natives:

(Beginning of Zinn's commentary.)

Arawak men and women, naked, tawny, and full of wonder, emerged from their villages onto the island's beaches and swam out to get a closer look at the strange big boat. When Columbus and his sailors came ashore, carrying swords, speaking oddly, the Arawaks ran to greet them, brought them food, water, gifts. He later wrote of this in his log:

For a recent example of these "secret combinations," *see* EJ Dickson, "Prayer, Politics and Power: 'The Family' Reveals Our Insidious American Theocracy," *RollingStone*, August 9, 2019, https://www.rollingstone.com/culture/culture-features/netflix-the-family-jesse-moss-secret-christian-cult-washington-dc-869396/.

[179] "Howard Zinn," *Wikipedia, The Free Encyclopedia*, last modified March 29, 2020, https://en.wikipedia.org/wiki/Howard_Zinn.

[180] "Christopher Columbus," *Wikipedia, The Free Encyclopedia*, last modified March 28, 2020, https://en.wikipedia.org/wiki/Christopher_Columbus.

"They ... brought us parrots and balls of cotton and spears and many other things, which they exchanged for the glass beads and hawks' bells. They willingly traded everything they owned... . They were well-built, with good bodies and handsome features. ... They do not bear arms, and do not know them, for I showed them a sword, they took it by the edge and cut themselves out of ignorance. They have no iron. Their spears are made of cane... . They would make fine servants. ... With fifty men we could subjugate them all and make them do whatever we want."

These Arawaks of the Bahama Islands were much like Indians on the mainland, who were remarkable (European observers were to say again and again) for their hospitality, their belief in sharing. These traits did not stand out in the Europe of the Renaissance, dominated as it was by the religion of popes, the government of kings, the frenzy for money that marked Western civilization and its first messenger to the Americas, Christopher Columbus.

Columbus wrote:

"As soon as I arrived in the Indies, on the first Island which I found, I took some of the natives by force in order that they might learn and might give me information of whatever there is in these parts."

The information that Columbus wanted most was: Where is the gold? He had persuaded the king and queen of Spain to finance an expedition to the lands, the wealth, he expected would be on the other side of the Atlantic-the Indies and Asia, gold and spices. For, like other informed people of his time, he knew the world was round and he could sail west in order to get to the Far East.

Spain was recently unified, one of the new modern nation-states, like France, England, and Portugal. Its population, mostly poor peasants, worked for the nobility, who were 2 percent of the population and owned 95 percent of the land. Spain had tied itself to the Catholic Church, expelled all the Jews, driven out the Moors.[181] Like other states of the modern world, Spain sought gold, which was becoming the new mark of wealth, more useful than land because it could buy anything.[182]

(End of Zinn's commentary.)

The great nations of Europe (mainly Great Britain, France, Spain, and Portugal) had access to raw materials

---

[181] "The Moors were the Muslim inhabitants of the Maghreb, the Iberian Peninsula, Sicily, and Malt during the Middle Ages." *See* "Moors," *Wikipedia, The Free Encyclopedia*, last modified April 4, 2020, https://en.wikipedia.org/wiki/Moors.

[182] Howard Zinn, *The People's History of the United States of America* (New York: Harper Perennial Modern Classics, 2005), 1–2, https://www.historyisaweapon.com/zinnapeopleshistory.html.

and goods in their respective foreign colonies.[183] This was the cause of the formation of this "great and abominable church."[184] These European nations began to transport slaves to their colonies, both from the new world (Western Hemisphere)[185] and from Africa.[186]

The vast lands that these European nations occupied outside of their domestic borders afforded them fertile land and access to their colonies' resources. To benefit from this, they needed slaves. These nations took advantage of innocent people, whom we call the "saints of God"[187] in our *new American scripture*, and forced many into slavery or killed them.[188]

---

[183] Leslie Kramer, "Mercantilism and the Colonies of Great Britain," *Investopedia*, June 26, 2019, https://www.investopedia.com/ask/answers/041615/how-did-mercantilism-affect-colonies-great-britain.asp.

[184] *See BOM*, 1 Nephi, chapters 13–14.

[185] Rebecca Onion, "America's Other Original Sin," *Slate*, January 18, 2016, http://www.slate.com/articles/news_and_politics/cover_story/2016/01/native_american_slavery_historians_uncover_a_chilling_chapter_in_u_s_history.html.

[186] "Britain and the Slave Trade," *The National Archives* (UK), accessed March 28, 2020, http://www.nationalarchives.gov.uk/slavery/pdf/britain-and-the-trade.pdf.

[187] *See BOM*, 1 Nephi 13:9.

[188] "How Slavery Helped Build a World Economy," *National Geographic*, January 3, 2003, https://www.nationalgeographic.com/news/2003/1/how-slavery-helped-build-a-world-economy/.

By the latter part of the 17th century, some of these nations established laws that made slavery a "fundamental and natural right"[189] of a white Christian. The foundation of Capitalism was beginning to be laid. The combination of the white Christian belief that their God would bless them with wealth and prosperity, along with their making as much money as possible through free market trade, was responsible for the establishment of these inhumane laws.

This is how we portrayed what was occurring in Europe in our new American scripture:

And it came to pass that I saw among the nations of the Gentiles [Europe] the formation of a great church. And the angel said unto me: Behold the formation of a church which is most abominable above all other churches, which slayeth the saints of God, yea, and tortureth them and bindeth them down, and yoketh them with a yoke of iron, and bringeth them down into captivity.

---

[189] Eric Eustice Williams, *Capitalism and Slavery*, (Chapel Hill: UNC Press, 1944), 32, https://archive.org/details/capitalismandsla033027mbp/page/n8/mode/2up.

And it came to pass that I beheld this great and abominable church; and I saw the devil that he was the founder of it. And I also saw gold, and silver, and silks, and scarlets, and fine-twined linen, and all manner of precious clothing; and I saw many harlots.

And the angel spake unto me, saying: Behold the gold, and the silver, and the silks, and the scarlets, and the fine-twined linen, and the precious clothing, and the harlots, are the desires of this great and abominable church. And also for the praise of the world do they destroy the saints of God, and bring them down into captivity.

And it came to pass that I looked and beheld many waters; and they divided the Gentiles from the seed of my brethren. And it came to pass that the angel said unto me: Behold the wrath of God is upon the seed of thy brethren [the native Americans].[190]

We covered this in our 1842 play:

LUCIFER: You can buy anything in this world for money.[191]

Our intent has always been to do good and to make our world a better place for all of humanity. As Zinn implied above, the European nations (of the Gentiles) had "tied [themselves in a secret combination of religious, political, and business powers] to the Catholic Church."[192] This secret combination was the basis of what we called the "great and abominable church of the devil."[193]

The native American cultures of South America were destroyed. Although two members of our group (the Real Illuminati™) were of ancient Incan descent, they found it

---

[190] *BOM*, 1 Nephi 13:4–11.
[191] *SNS*, Chapter 5, 85–113.
[192] Zinn, *People's History*, 2.
[193] See *BOM*, 1 Nephi, chapters 13–14.

very difficult to work within the Spanish and Portuguese colonies that were developing there. They found none who had the same "intent to do good"[194] as we did. By the end of the 16th century, these two members of our group had traveled to Europe and ended up in England.

Not mentioned in the orthodox history presented to American citizens of the United States is how the first government in the New World (North America) was established.

This is how it happened:

The British crown picked a council of men to govern its newly established American colonies.

The names of seven men, chosen by the court of the King of England, were kept secret and sealed in a box. The box was not to be opened until the ships carrying the men—who were commissioned to establish a colonial government—arrived in the New World. These names were kept secret in order to avoid mutiny by the men who did all the work—not only while they were on the ships

---

[194] *BOM*, Jacob 2:19.

carrying them across the Atlantic Ocean, but also once they arrived. These laborers were needed to construct the buildings at Jamestown—the first American colony.

In a new land away from the Crown's soldiers, a majority (the people doing all the work) could have easily overwhelmed and killed the minority. The working men didn't know whose names were part of the first American secret combination. Because these laborers thought that their own names could possibly be one of the seven, this hope kept them under control.

Once the names *were* revealed,[195] it was very evident to the majority that the few names were those who were the wealthiest men with the greatest economic influence, working secretly for, and on behalf of, the Crown.

Once in the new land, the majority of laborers believed it was in their best interest to allow the few to do what the few do best. They trusted the few to create an economic structure that would work for everyone, not just for the few, but for the majority ... so they hoped and were promised anyway.

---

[195] *See* "The Jamestown Chronicles Timeline," *The Jamestown Chronicles*, 2007, https://www.historyisfun.org/sites/jamestown-chronicles/timeline.html.

While living and working in England at that time, two of our group (the Real Illuminati™) were employed by the Christopher Fox family. While employed with the Fox family, we came to know the Anthony Gosnold family, with whom Fox engaged in business affairs. While working with the Foxes and the Gosnolds, we came to know two Gosnold sons, Anthony Jr. and Bartholomew.[196]

Having been secretly chosen as one of the *Secret Seven*, Bartholomew entrusted us with his secret. He did this because he believed that we were simple and illiterate. (We presented ourselves as such in order to be trusted and do what we could to influence change.) Bartholomew asked us to accompany him and his brother to the New World as laborers. This was our intent.

Christopher Fox was a cloth maker by trade. He was always looking for cheaper raw materials to make his clothing. The Gosnold sons promised cheaper materials from the New World. This is what influenced Fox to agree to allow the two of us (who worked for Fox) to accompany

---

[196] "Bartholomew Gosnold," *Wikipedia, The Free Encyclopedia*, last modified November 27, 2019, https://en.wikipedia.org/wiki/Bartholomew_Gosnold.

the Gosnold sons to America. (As we explained in the first book of our Trilogy, we become servants in order to influence others.)[197]

Our intent was to do good. It has always been our intent to do good ... for the majority.

It soon became very apparent to us that there was only one *true* purpose, and one purpose only, for the new American colonies: "gold, and the silver, and silks, and scarlets, and fine-twined linen, and all manner of precious clothing."[198]

The two of us who traveled to America with the Gosnold sons were still employed by Christopher Fox, and therefore returned again to England. Christopher Fox had a son named George Fox.[199]

When he was of age, George worked alongside us (referring to the two we have mentioned) almost every day. By our presence, we were able to greatly influence his intellectual growth. The Fox family treated us well; and

---

[197] *See THOR* (large print), 274–8.

[198] *BOM*, 1 Nephi 13:7.

[199] "George Fox," *Wikipedia, The Free Encyclopedia*, last modified March 11, 2020, https://en.wikipedia.org/wiki/George_Fox.

although we were just laborers, George came to see us as his friends, similar to how a nephew might see his uncles.

The Fox family was very religious—one of the most sincere and devoted Christian families we had ever encountered. George was very gregarious (social, outgoing) and smart. In his teens, he would often debate men much older than him about religion, politics, and the events of that time. George began to see the great divisions and hypocrisy of the Protestant religions. As he grew, his intelligence and common sense eventually attracted quite a following.

It wasn't long before George was encountering a lot of persecution. This not only got him jailed on many occasions, but inspired him to search for a place where he could live religion freely, as he and those who listened to him believed.

When we wrote the storyline for our *new American scripture* (the *Book of Mormon*), we used our knowledge and experience from George's life. We wanted to express what often happened to many European-Christians of that time period when they encountered persecution for standing up against the prevailing authorities of their nations.

George Fox had encountered and fought against the political, economic, and religious powers that had secretly combined to form what we called in our story, a "great and abominable church."[200]

In our new American scripture, we would later write:

And I looked and beheld a man among the Gentiles, who was separated from the seed of my brethren by the many waters; and I beheld the Spirit of God, that it came down and wrought upon the man; and he went forth upon the many waters, even unto the seed of my brethren, who were in the promised land. And it came to pass that I beheld the Spirit of God, that it wrought upon other Gentiles; and they went forth out of captivity, upon the many waters.[201]

---

[200] *BOM*, 1 Nephi 13:4–9.
[201] *BOM*, 1 Nephi 13:12–13.

The modern Mormons deceive the world and present the "man among the Gentiles"[202] as Christopher Columbus. The man to whom we actually referred couldn't have been any more different from Columbus. Honest history reports that Columbus certainly didn't possess "the Spirit of God."[203]

The man we were referring to was George Fox, who, more than any other religious leader, tried to promote equality and fairness in the early American colonies, and among the native Americans.

On September 18, 1793, in Washington, D.C., George Washington laid the cornerstone for the United States Capitol building.[204] In this building, a new nation would form the laws that would govern its people for many future generations. George Washington was wearing an apron when he laid the cornerstone.[205] It was the same apron that

---

[202] *BOM*, 1 Nephi 13:13.

[203] *BOM*, 1 Nephi 13:13. *See also* Zinn, *People's History*, 2.

[204] *Centennial Anniversary of the Laying of the Corner-Stone of the National Capitol, September 18, 1793* (Washington, D.C.: Capitol Centennial Committee, 1893), 7, https://archive.org/details/centennialanniv00usgoog/page/n11/mode/2up/search/apron.

[205] "George Washington's Masonic Apron on View," *Mount Vernon Ladies' Association*, accessed April 3, 2020, https://www.mountvernon.org/plan-your-visit/calendar/exhibitions/george-washington-s-masonic-apron-on-view/.

Freemasons wore when they perform their secret rituals.[206] (This was also the same apron that we used in our 1842 play to dress out the Lucifer character.)[207]

For many years, the U.S. Capitol building was used each Sunday for religious services. This upset a few of the Founding Fathers, who had fought hard to keep government separated from religion.

This was also of great concern to us.

Behind the scenes, we had been involved in influencing two of the most influential (yet generally unpopular) U.S. Founding Fathers: Thomas Paine[208] and Ethan Allen.[209] They were part of the group of men that met to discuss the creation of the United States Constitution. Although many of the Founding Fathers refused to neglect or set aside their Christian beliefs, the

---

Jason Williams, "The Gift," *The George Washington Masonic Cave*, November 26, 2018, https://georgewashingtoncave.org/2018/11/26/the-gift/.

[206] "Freemasonry," *Wikipedia, The Free Encyclopedia*, last modified March 20, 2020, https://en.wikipedia.org/wiki/Freemasonry.

[207] *SNS*, 51–4.

[208] "Thomas Paine," *Wikipedia, The Free Encyclopedia*, last modified March 29, 2020, https://en.wikipedia.org/wiki/Thomas_Paine.

[209] "Ethan Allen," *Wikipedia, The Free Encyclopedia*, last modified March 25, 2020, https://en.wikipedia.org/wiki/Ethan_Allen.

sound reasoning and logic of Paine and Allen greatly influenced some of the other men to ensure a secure separation of church and state.

Throughout the years that followed, the United States Congress began to legislate (create laws) according to the Representatives' and Senators' religious beliefs. These American political leaders largely ignored the Constitution that had established a Congress for the people and by the people, and that had properly separated church and state.

After the United States of America gained its independence and set up its own government, the American people began to prosper unlike any other newly created nation in recorded history. After its Founding Fathers agreed upon a Constitution that replaced the colonies' Articles of Confederation,[210] we were greatly saddened, because of the deception that the few created for the majority.

---

[210] "Articles of Confederation," *Wikipedia, The Free Encyclopedia*, last modified March 19, 2020, https://en.wikipedia.org/wiki/Articles_of_Confederation.

When the new Constitution was accepted, it did not include the right for women, native Americans, slaves, or white men who didn't own any property to vote. The various States each made their own suffrage (voting) laws. The original Constitution did not specifically outline a person's rights under law.

It also did not include a Senate in Congress. The reason that the Founders amended the original Constitution to include Senators was so that the wealthy of each State would be properly represented.[211] Democracy—the rule of the majority—has never really been part of American politics and government (regardless of what the people may believe). If the majority 51% ruled, the 49% minority (including "the few") would surely be crushed and controlled.

The wealthy have always been the minority (the few). The wealthy didn't want poor people interfering with their wealth, or governing them. The wealthy ran the States, in spite of what the newly created Federal

---

[211] *See THOR* (large print), xxvi–xxviii ("Introduction," 26–8).

Government of the United States of America purported to want. The states of America were never united. The Civil War resulted because of this division.

The majority has always been deceived by the minority. The wealthy felt that the poor did not have the same will and intent in government that they had. Being poor meant that the majority might be tempted to vote for gain, taking from the rich. Some wealthy merchants argued hypocritically[212] (deceitfully) that if men who didn't own land *were* allowed to vote, their votes could easily be purchased/swayed for a few dollars, or to maintain their employment that was provided by the wealthy. White men who didn't own property could not vote for many years.

And it would be even many more years until darker-skinned people and women were granted the ability to vote. Much later, there was a movement to allow women to vote in the Wyoming Territory,[213] but the movement had a

---

[212] Definition: "Characterized by behavior that contradicts what one claims to believe or feel; characterized by hypocrisy." *See* "hypocritical," in *Merriam-Webster Dictionary*, accessed April 4, 2020, https://www.merriam-webster.com/dictionary/hypocritically.

[213] "Wyoming Territory," *Wikipedia, The Free Encyclopedia*, last modified March 28, 2020, https://en.wikipedia.org/wiki/Wyoming_Territory.

nefarious intent.[214] After slavery was outlawed by the Federal Government, the men living in Wyoming wanted to protect their land from being overrun by newly liberated slaves. To increase their chances of controlling local laws and authority—solely to control their land and keep it from being controlled by unwanted others—women living in Wyoming were allowed to vote with their husbands.

In the new Utah Territory, Mormons saw the benefit of the women in Wyoming having the right to vote. They quickly adopted their own territorial laws to protect their religious rights granted by local law and authority. If a man had seven wives, that man now had eight votes.

It has always been our hope that Americans would do good. As we observed what kind of governments the European immigrants to America were establishing, we realized that something had to be done to influence a fairer and "more perfect Union."[215]

---

[214] Definition: "Evil, or dishonest." *See* "nefarious," in *Macmillan English Dictionary*, accessed April 4, 2020, https://www.macmillandictionary.com/dictionary/american/nefarious#nefarious_3.

[215] "Preamble, We the People," *Interactive Constitution*, accessed March 29, 2020, https://constitutioncenter.org/interactive-constitution/preamble.

Our intent was contrary to the intent of the wealthy. The few had deceived the majority by promoting the American Declaration of Independence. Countering this deception was part of our intent in writing our new scripture (the *Book of Mormon*). Its storyline impresses upon the reader just how much good America *could* do for the world. It also warns Americans what will happen if they choose to do evil.[216]

Here is a Real Truth that often angers the rest of the world, but cannot be disputed:

If not for the involvement of the United States of America in the European conflict known as World War II,[217] most, if not all, of the Eastern Hemisphere would have eventually been controlled by Germany.

After World War II, the United States basically controlled the world. As a direct result of that war, the United States set up the World Bank[218] and the

---

[216] *BOM*, 1 Nephi 14:7.

[217] "World War II," *Wikipedia, The Free Encyclopedia*, last modified March 20, 2020, https://en.wikipedia.org/wiki/World_War_II.

[218] "World Bank," *Wikipedia, The Free Encyclopedia*, last modified March 27, 2020, https://en.wikipedia.org/wiki/World_Bank.

International Monetary Fund[219], the legal structures that control the modern world's economies. Without the help of the United States and its economic policies and industry, Europe could not have rebounded from the devastation it experienced during World War II.

This is *real* power and influence. This is great power. This has set the United States of America "above all other nations"[220] on Earth. Bar none!

In the first book of our Trilogy—*The True History of Religion*—we explained how the United States was the first government on Earth (during this current dispensation of time) to possess the knowledge and ability associated with nuclear (atomic) power.[221]

As atoms are the building blocks of all matter, in a religious sense, atoms can be referred to as "God's" building blocks. God uses His power ... the power in these building

---

[219] "International Monetary Fund," *Wikipedia, The Free Encyclopedia*, last modified March 29, 2020, https://en.wikipedia.org/wiki/International_Monetary_Fund.

[220] *BOM*, 1 Nephi 13:30.

[221] "Nuclear power," *Wikipedia, The Free Encyclopedia*, last modified March 19, 2020, https://en.wikipedia.org/wiki/Nuclear_power.

blocks ... to create all things. It can be said that the "power of God"[222] is nuclear energy.

In our first book, we explained how we were able to influence certain scientists living in Europe to solve the puzzle of nuclear energy in order to control it and use it for human purposes.[223] We were indirectly responsible for influencing these European scientists to give the knowledge to the Americans.[224]

These scientists lived in countries that were quickly being overcome and occupied by Hitler's military forces. Had these scientists *not* given their knowledge to America, it would have fallen under Hitler's[225] power and control. This would have changed the entire course of history, and the world would not be the place it is today.

We knew of this power long before these scientists did.

In the course of our writings, we have presented and will present details about Earth's past history, which will

---

[222] *BOM*, 1 Nephi 13:18–19, 30.

[223] *THOR* (large print), 48–51.

[224] *THOR* (large print), 49.

[225] "Adolf Hitler," *Wikipedia, The Free Encyclopedia*, last modified March 29, 2020, https://en.wikipedia.org/wiki/Adolf_Hitler.

include details about how other great ancient civilizations, that once existed and were destroyed by nuclear energy, used this energy for weapons of destruction.

How can we prove this? By using logic and reason.

Consider the most arid (driest) place on Earth: the Atacama Desert located in Chile, South America.[226]

This desert is located in the coastal regions of South America. Early explorers found that most coastal regions of the world were lush with vegetation and had a climate that was comfortable for human habitation. As they do today, ancient humans migrated to the best parts of the world to live.

The Atacama Desert was once the location of the most prosperous and thriving metropolitan cities of its time period. Ancient humans congregated in the Atacama region and developed a huge urban development, where more than a billion people lived in a very concentrated, highly advanced urban metropolis.

---

[226] "Atacama Desert," *Wikipedia, The Free Encyclopedia*, last modified March 29, 2020, https://en.wikipedia.org/wiki/Atacama_Desert.

Consider the ideas that current science fiction writers present about highly advanced futuristic cities that are clean and able to house many people in just a small area. To create these cities, all the natural vegetation had to be removed. Vegetation needs water. Earth's natural laws, when considered as they exist, make sure that water is available to the areas of the earth that have vegetation. The great rainforests of Earth give evidence of this.

If humans were to remove all the vegetation from a rainforest and build a huge city, the amount of rain falling in that area would eventually naturally decrease proportionately and exponentially.[227]

Using the modern word *Atacama* as a name for this ancient city, the city of Atacama was one of the most advanced and prosperous cities on Earth at that time.

Long story short ... civil war broke out and advanced nuclear weapons, which were available to both sides of

---

[227] Lauren Morello, "Cutting Down Rainforests Also Cuts Down on Rainfall," *Scientific American*, September 6, 2012, https://www.scientificamerican.com/article/cutting-down-rainforests/;

"Vegetation: Its Role in Weather and Climate," *North Carolina Climate Office*, accessed March 29, 2020, https://climate.ncsu.edu/edu/Vegetation.

the conflict, completely annihilated Atacama and all of its people.

There were a few people who escaped "into the wilderness,"[228] but these remaining enclaves of people did not have the knowledge necessary to rebuild the city. The descendants of those who survived hardly knew anything about the technology that was destroyed. Furthermore, they didn't have access to any of the books that contained this knowledge.

Over millions of years, the modern Atacama Desert is the aftermath of total nuclear destruction. In fact, most places of modern Earth that are deserts are a result of the same thing: ancient civilizations completely destroyed by nuclear war, because of the misuse of the "power of God."[229]

As we have explained throughout our writings, we (the Real Illuminati™) have a lot of Real Truth to share with this world. But if we cannot influence humanity to set aside

---

[228] *See* 1 Nephi 2:2; Mosiah 24:20; and Alma 27:14 for just a few examples of people fleeing "into the wilderness" in the *Book of Mormon. See also THOR,* 39.
[229] *BOM,* 1 Nephi 13:18–19, 30.

its differences and unite as one people on Earth, what good will sharing the Real Truth about ancient Earth do?

Our *new American scripture* was meant for Americans (the nation of the United States of America). Our story is not about the rest of the world. Our story is *about* America, the most powerful and influential nation in the current dispensation of human time. Our story was not meant for other nations, nor for other people. Our story was meant for the nation that would save the world from Nazi fascism. Our story was meant for the nation that *can* end poverty and establish equity throughout this world, if they will.

Nevertheless, our story and its message have been rejected and transfigured by the Americans, where *transfigured* means: given a new meaning and transformed outwardly to present something that we did not intend.

In every sense of the word *fascism*, the United States of America is the most fascist nation on Earth and has placed itself above all other nations. The proper definition of *fascism* is "extreme nationalism that promotes the interests of one nation or people above all others."[230] The United States of America promotes itself and supports itself very similarly to how Nazi Germany did. "America the Beautiful"[231] is the most fascist nation on Earth ... bar none!

In our new scripture, we warned the Americans (Gentiles) about what would happen if they failed to accept our message, and instead, followed their pride and ego (i.e. *Lucifer*). First, we introduced the United States of America as a people "who have gone forth out of captivity."[232] Leaving this "captivity" refers to America's revolutionary war against Great Britain:

> And I beheld their mother Gentiles were gathered
> together upon the waters, and upon the land also,
> to battle against them.[233]

---

[230] *Compare* "Ultranationalism," *Wikipedia, The Free Encyclopedia*, last modified April 4, 2020, https://en.wikipedia.org/wiki/Ultranationalism.

[231] "Patriotwritr," "America the Beautiful (performed by the Mormon Tabernacle Choir)," *YouTube*, December 3, 2008, https://www.youtube.com/watch?v=Rzs52OzgWOs.

[232] *BOM*, 1 Nephi 13:13, 16, 29–30.

[233] *BOM*, 1 Nephi 13:17.

In our story, we reiterated that the "power of God" was with the Americans, and that this "power" caused the United States to have the most powerful military on Earth:

> And I beheld that the power of God was with them, and also that the wrath of God was upon all those that were gathered together against them to battle ... that the Gentiles that had gone out of captivity [won their Revolutionary War[234] and] were delivered by the power of God out of the hands of all other nations. ... the Gentiles who have gone forth out of captivity, and have been lifted up by the power of God above all other nations.[235]

Our story explains that God was with the Americans; that God blessed them and gave them the "power of God"[236]

---

[234] History.com Editors, "Revolutionary War," *History.com*, last modified September 3, 2019, https://www.history.com/topics/american-revolution/american-revolution-history.

[235] *BOM*, 1 Nephi 13:18–19, 30.

[236] *BOM*, 1 Nephi 13:18–19, 30.

to make the United States the most powerful and greatest nation "above all other nations."[237]

The United States of America has become the most industrious and wealthy nation in contemporary-recorded history. Americans have given all the credit to their God; however, it is actually the "god of this world."[238]

In our new American scripture, we attempted to impress upon the mind of the reader how religious people feel when, through their industry and hard work, they begin to prosper more than other people in the world do. When this happens, religious people believe that they are being "blessed" by God, while all others, who do not believe as they do, are being "cursed." Actually, their prosperity is from their hard work alone and how they use Capitalism for their advantage, the advantage of the few.

This belief was also held by the ancient Hebrews.[239]

To counter this erroneous belief that the Jews held during that time period, knowing it would result in more

---

[237] *BOM*, 1 Nephi 13:30.
[238] *See BOM*, Mosiah 3:19; *see also SNS*, 87.
[239] Christopher, "Jewish & LDS (Mormon) Parallels," *Marvelous Work and a Wonder*®, 2010, www.pearlpublishing.net/tsp/download/JewishLDSParallels.4.4.20.pdf.

division and misery in the world, we helped Socrates to write the words of Isaiah. When read in context, Isaiah's words condemn organized religious practices: "vain oblations, incense, sabbaths, and the calling of assemblies [church meetings]."[240] Isaiah's words also attempt to influence believers to "learn to do well; seek judgment, relieve the oppressed, judge the fatherless, plead for the widow."[241]

As we contemplated how we were going to write our new American scripture, we considered what had happened with the Hebrews. We considered the time period and the events surrounding the rise of their culture and religion, as well as what their religious pride had done.

Our book, the *Book of Mormon*, incorporates a large part of the book of Isaiah into its storyline. Upon writing our modern new American scripture, we made sure that the significance and importance of Isaiah's words were clearly understood:

---

[240] *Compare* Isaiah 1:13.
[241] Isaiah 1:17.

And now, behold, I say unto you, that ye ought to search these things. Yea, a commandment I give unto you that ye search these things diligently; for great are the words of Isaiah.

For surely he spake as touching all things concerning my people which are of the house of Israel; therefore it must needs be that he must speak also to the Gentiles.

And all things that he spake have been and shall be, even according to the words which he spake.

Therefore give heed to my words; write the things which I have told you; and according to the time and the will of the Father they shall go forth unto the Gentiles.[242]

---

[242] *BOM*, 3 Nephi 23:1–4.

The book of Isaiah wasn't the only Old Testament scripture that we inspired. Throughout the storyline of our new American scripture, we gave clues about how our new story dovetailed (united) with the Hebrew Old Testament.

We began our story (the *Book of Mormon*) at the same time period when the Hebrew culture was destroyed by the Babylonians (circa 600 BCE).[243] We knew that much of ancient Jewish history could be disputed. But this particular event could not.

About this we wrote:

> And now I would that ye should know, that even since the days of Abraham there have been many prophets that have testified these things; yea, behold, the prophet Zenos did testify boldly; for the which he was slain.

> And behold, also Zenock, and also Ezias, and also Isaiah, and Jeremiah, (Jeremiah being that same

---

[243] "Babylonian captivity," *Wikipedia, The Free Encyclopedia*, last modified April 3, 2020, https://en.wikipedia.org/wiki/Babylonian_captivity. *See also BOM*, Introduction.

prophet who testified of the destruction of Jerusalem) and now we know that Jerusalem was destroyed according to the words of Jeremiah. O then why not the Son of God come, according to his prophecy?

And now will you dispute that Jerusalem was destroyed? Will ye say that the sons of Zedekiah were not slain, all except it were Mulek? Yea, and do ye not behold that the seed of Zedekiah are with us, and they were driven out of the land of Jerusalem?[244]

When our book was actually *published* in 1830, it did not include the most important chapter of Isaiah—chapter 1. That chapter was part of our original storyline, but we were forced to rewrite after it was peer reviewed (116-page lost manuscript).[245] For this reason, the prophets

---

[244] *BOM*, Helaman 8:19–21.
[245] *See TSP*, Appendix 2, "The Book of Lehi; The Lost 116-Page Manuscript," 591–633.

Zenos and Zenock, which are not Old Testament prophets, but were introduced in our original *book of Lehi*,[246] are mentioned in the 1830 edition. The teachings of Zenos and Zenock are mentioned throughout the storyline.

As you consider why and how we wrote the *Book of Mormon* for the early American Christians, it is important to consider how and for what purpose every aspect of the story was created. In the 1830 edition, the quotes from Isaiah start with Isaiah chapter 2, and use, in sequence, chapters 3 through 14, and a few other important parts of Isaiah.

Isaiah, chapter 14 ends on the premise for which we not only wrote the original book of Isaiah to confound the Hebrews, but also for which we wrote the new scripture to inspire the Americans (Gentiles):

What shall one then answer the messengers of the nation? That the LORD hath founded Zion, and the poor of his people shall trust in it.[247]

---

[246] *TSP*, 591.
[247] Isaiah 14:32; *Compare BOM*, 2 Nephi 24:32.

Our intent in writing a new American scripture was to inspire the European Christians to establish a "New Jerusalem" (Zion) in the United States of America, a nation "above all other nations" on Earth ... IN WHICH THE POOR PEOPLE COULD TRUST.

But our story also explains that there was only ONE REASON and ONE REASON only, for God making America great—"for the intent to do good."[248]

We illustrated this by pointing out what the Americans *could* do for the native American peoples, about whom the *Book of Mormon* was written.

In our story, the native Americans—and others of the world's disenfranchised and marginalized people, i.e., "the more part of all the tribes have been led away; and they are scattered to and fro upon the isles of the sea"[249]—are *supposed to be* "nursed by the Gentiles":

---

[248] *BOM*, Jacob 2:19.
[249] *BOM*, 1 Nephi 22:4.

Nevertheless, after they shall be *nursed* by the Gentiles, and the Lord has lifted up his hand upon the Gentiles and set them up for a standard [as the ultimate standard of one who *nurses*, i.e., a mother], and their children have been carried in their arms [what mothers do], and their daughters have been carried upon their shoulders, behold these things of which are spoken are temporal [worldly things—the basic necessities of life—versus *spiritual* things]; ... that the Lord God will raise up a mighty nation among the Gentiles, yea, even upon the face of this land; and by them shall our seed be scattered [Americans scattering the native Americans].

And after our seed is scattered the Lord God will proceed to do a *marvelous work among the Gentiles*, which shall be of great worth unto our seed; wherefore, it is likened unto their being nourished by the Gentiles and being carried in their arms and upon their shoulders.[250]

This "marvelous work among the Gentiles"[251] that we had hoped would be done by the Americans was supposed to be *temporal* as opposed to *spiritual* things.

A good mother provides temporal security and the temporal things that a child needs: food, clothing, shelter, healthcare, and education. Instead of becoming a mother figure to the native American people (both of North and South America) and setting up a "marvelous work" ... "for the intent to do good,"[252] the Americans transfigured our scripture and made our message *spiritual*, instead of *temporal*.

By transfiguring our message, the Americans eventually established one of the wealthiest religions on Earth.[253] Instead of using our new American scripture to "nurse" the native American peoples, as any loving mother

---

[250] *Compare BOM*, 1 Nephi 22:6–8, emphasis added.

[251] *See* answer under "Does the Real Illuminati™ have anything to do with COVID-19?" *Real Illuminati™*, accessed April 5, 2020, https://www.realilluminati.org/faq-s.

[252] *BOM*, Jacob 2:19.

[253] *Wikipedia*, "List of wealthiest organizations."

would, the Conservative Republican-based Church of Jesus Christ of Latter-day Saints supports political policies that secure the southern borders of the United States[254] that repel "our seed."[255]

Instead of acting as a mother to the native American peoples, as well as to those whom we referred to in our storyline as the "lost [ten] tribes"[256] (marginalized and disenfranchised) ... "the tired, the poor, the huddled masses yearning to breathe free, the wretched refuse of your teeming shore,"[257] Mormons put themselves up as the *spiritual* standard to the world.[258]

---

[254] "We acknowledge that every nation has the right to enforce its laws and secure its borders." *See* "Church Supports Principles of *Utah Compact* on Immigration," *The Church of Jesus Christ of Latter-day Saints*, November 11, 2010, https://newsroom.churchofjesuschrist.org/article/church-supports-principles-of-utah-compact-on-immigration.

    See also "Immigration: Church Issues New Statement," *The Church of Jesus Christ of Latter-day Saints*, June 10, 2011, https://newsroom.churchofjesuschrist.org/article/immigration-church-issues-new-statement: "Most Americans agree that the federal government of the United States should secure its borders and sharply reduce or eliminate the flow of undocumented immigrants. "

[255] *BOM*, 1 Nephi 22:8.

[256] *BOM*, 3 Nephi 21:26–9; 3 Nephi 17:4; 2 Nephi 29:14.

[257] *Compare* "The New Colossus," *Wikipedia, The Free Encyclopedia*, last modified March 13, 2020, http://en.wikipedia.org/wiki/The_New_Colossus.

[258] "The Church of Jesus Christ of Latter-day Saints," *The Church of Jesus Christ of Latter-day Saints*, accessed March 29, 2020, https://www.churchofjesuschrist.org.

The secret combination of America's religious, political, and business powers causes "the blood of saints [to] cry unto the Lord."[259]

In our story, we presented a prophecy that we had hoped would become self-fulfilling—when the Gentiles nurse the people and carry them in their arms and upon their shoulders.[260] In this prophecy, we were unwavering in explaining that "the eternal purposes of the Lord shall roll on, until all his promises shall be fulfilled."[261]

We told the readers to "search the prophecies of Isaiah."[262] The first chapter of Isaiah renounces religious ordinances, rituals, meetings, and everything else upon which the modern LDS/Mormon religion places a great *spiritual* emphasis. Contrasting this, *we* (the Real Illuminati™) were trying to get them to use their *temporal* wealth to become a standard of the best "nursing mother" on Earth.

---

[259] *BOM*, Mormon 8:27, 41.
[260] *BOM*, 1 Nephi 22:6.
[261] *BOM*, Mormon 8:22.
[262] *BOM*, Mormon 8:23.

After Isaiah renounces the *spiritual things* about a religion, he emphasizes *temporal things*. Isaiah asks religious people to "make you clean; put away the evil of your doings."[263] These "evil doings" are the same "doings" that we had our Jesus Christ show unto our character Moroni, the son of Mormon, when he said, "I know your doing."[264]

Isaiah tells religious people to "cease to do evil; learn to do well; seek judgment, relieve the oppressed, judge the fatherless, plead for the widow."[265]

There are few other humans on Earth as oppressed as those trying to get into the United States of America from South America,[266] those who are tired, those who are poor, those who are huddled masses yearning to breathe free, and the wretched refuse of other nations' teeming shores.[267]

---

[263] Isaiah 1:16.

[264] *See BOM*, Mormon, chapter 8.

[265] Isaiah 1:16–17.

[266] "Fleeing For Our Lives: Central American Migrant Crisis," *Amnesty International*, accessed March 29, 2020, https://www.amnestyusa.org/fleeing-for-our-lives-central-american-migrant-crisis/.

See *also* Daniel Gonzalez, "The 2019 migrant surge is unlike any we've seen before. This is why," *USA Today*, September 25, 2019, https://www.usatoday.com/in-depth/news/nation/2019/09/23/immigration-issues-migrants-mexico-central-america-caravans-smuggling/2026215001/.

[267] "The New Colossus," https://en.wikipedia.org/wiki/The_New_Colossus.

The greatest nation on Earth, a nation that became what it is because of the "power of God"[268] that has upheld it, supported it, and made it what it is, has become the MOST EVIL NATION ON EARTH ... bar none.

We did everything in our power, and will continue to do what we can, to help the Americans become the appropriate "standard" that this nation was meant to be.

The United States of America was meant to be a mother who nurses her children and carries them in her arms and upon her shoulders. But the children whom this mother should be nurturing and caring for, are instead "cry[ing] unto the Lord."[269]

As we wrote and warned the Gentiles in our new American scripture, the cries of the righteous shall no longer be ignored.[270] The same "wrath of God"[271] that was against all nations that rose up against the United States of America—the same "power of God"[272] that made America

---

[268] *BOM*, 1 Nephi 13:18–19, 30.
[269] *BOM*, Mormon 8:23, 27, 40.
[270] *BOM*, Mormon 8:41. *See also* Proverbs 1:24–5.
[271] *BOM*, 1 Nephi 22:16.
[272] *BOM*, 1 Nephi 13:18–19, 30.

the greatest nation "above all nations"[273]—shall be used *against* these Gentiles, according to what we have written:

> For the time soon cometh that the fulness of the wrath of God shall be poured out upon all the children of men; for he will not suffer that the wicked shall destroy the righteous.[274]

> Behold, the sword of vengeance hangeth over you; and the time soon cometh that he avengeth the blood of the saints upon you, for he will not suffer their cries any longer.[275]

The "power of God"[276] as we have explained it is the availability of nuclear technology. The "wrath of God"[277] is the absence of "God's" intervention.[278] It is just a matter of time

---

[273] *BOM*, 1 Nephi 13:30. *See also BOM*, 3 Nephi 16:10.
[274] *BOM*, 1 Nephi 22:16.
[275] *BOM*, Mormon 8:41.
[276] *BOM*, 1 Nephi 13:18–19, 30.
[277] *BOM*, 1 Nephi 14:15–17.
[278] *See THOR* (large print), Chapter 12. *See also 666 America*, 28–31, 167–8, 418, 447.

before nuclear weapons will be as accessible as other weapons that are used by those who the Gentiles call "terrorists." Before terrorist groups acquire nuclear capabilities, we have intervened in other ways to hopefully inspire change in American policy. For this intent, COVID-19[279] was introduced throughout the world.[280] With a wise purpose, this pandemic affects the United States more than any nation on Earth.

As we publish this introduction to our upcoming book, *A New American Scripture*,[281] the coronavirus pandemic[282] is challenging the "great and abominable church of the devil"[283] (Capitalism). This is another portend (signal) of the "wrath of God."[284] We have the knowledge of how this

---

[279] "Coronavirus disease 2019, *Wikipedia, The Free Encyclopedia*, last modified April 6, 2020, https://en.wikipedia.org/wiki/Coronavirus_disease_2019.

[280] "Does the Real Illuminati™ have anything to do with COVID-19?" *Real Illuminati*™, accessed April 5, 2020, https://www.realilluminati.org/faq-s.

[281] "A New American Scripture," *Real Illuminati*™, accessed March 29, 2020, https://www.realilluminati.org/a-new-american-scripture-u1xei.

[282] "Coronavirus," *World Health Organization*, WHO, accessed March 29, 2020, https://www.who.int/health-topics/coronavirus#tab=tab_1.

[283] *See BOM*, 1 Nephi, chapter 14.

[284] *BOM*, 1 Nephi 22:16.

pandemic started and how it can end.[285] However, withholding our knowledge and help from the world will cause this world to stumble enough, we hope, to open the hearts and minds of humanity to the "intent to do good."[286]

As the world's economic structure collapses because of the pandemic, governments will produce new money to save it. In so doing, governments will be forced to use this new money to provide the basic necessities of life to all of humanity—proving that this "intent to do good" *can be done*.

Unfortunately, once the pandemic is over, there is a high probability that the "great and abominable church of the devil"[287] will once again continue to wreak havoc upon the poor and the needy people of the world. If the world fails to learn from this pandemic demonstration of the "wrath of God,"[288] there will be a few other events that cause humanity to reflect on what it is going to take to make life upon Earth compatible and fair for all humans.[289]

---

[285] "How are plagues, like the current COVID-19, good for humanity?" *Real Illuminati*™, accessed April 7, 2020, https://www.realilluminati.org/faq-s.

[286] *BOM*, Jacob 2:19.

[287] *See BOM*, 1 Nephi, chapter 14.

[288] *BOM*, 1 Nephi 22:16.

[289] "One Race, One People, One World," https://www.realilluminati.org.

Natural cataclysmic events associated with earthquakes, volcanos, hurricanes, asteroids, and other natural events will be next. If these natural events fail to create a united world with the "intent to do good,"[290] we will allow another devastating blow to the world's economy: the disruption of the world's electronic infrastructure upon which the "great and abominable church of the devil"[291] is dependent.

A portend (foreshadowing) of this occurred in 1859. A great solar storm disrupted the electronic transmissions being used at the time to connect the world.[292]

In our new American scripture (the *Book of Mormon*), we presented an example of this in one of the allegories used to note the "wrath of God,"[293] in hopes of waking up humanity. It was a subtle warning to a world that was, at that time, relying upon the new industrial and technological advancements, but not for the right reasons.

---

[290] *BOM*, Jacob 2:19.

[291] *See BOM*, 1 Nephi, chapter 14.

[292] "Solar storm of 1859," *Wikipedia, The Free Encyclopedia*, last modified March 20, 2020, https://en.wikipedia.org/wiki/Solar_storm_of_1859.

[293] *BOM*, 1 Nephi 22:16.

We wrote of three days of complete darkness, during which no one could light a fire or create any other source of artificial light.[294]

If these events still fail to wake up humanity, one last *non-intervention* will take place. We will not intervene in terrorist groups acquiring nuclear weapons. We will not aid them, but we will *not* do what we have done for many years, which is to secretly report what we know to government agencies. These agencies are set up to mitigate (lessen) the frequency of terrorists acquiring and using nuclear technology.

We used another name for these "terrorists" in our *Book of Mormon*. We called them "a remnant of the house of Jacob."[295] We were very clear what would happen if the Gentiles "do not repent after the blessing which they shall receive, after they have scattered my people."[296]

---

[294] *BOM*, 3 Nephi, chapter 8.
[295] *BOM*, 3 Nephi 20:16.
[296] *BOM*, 3 Nephi 20:15–17; 21:12.

We warned them, "Wo be unto the Gentiles except they repent."[297]

After our Jesus delivered unto the people "the fulness of the everlasting Gospel,"[298] we had our Jesus warn the Gentiles about what would happen if they "do not repent"[299] after receiving such a great blessing—referring to the words that Jesus taught to both the Jews[300] and to the ancient inhabitants of the Western Hemisphere.[301]

Our Jesus warned them:

And my people who are a remnant of Jacob shall be among the Gentiles, yea, in the midst of them as a lion among the beasts of the forest, as a young lion among the flocks of sheep, who, if he go through both treadeth down and teareth in pieces, and none can deliver. Their hand shall be lifted up upon their adversaries,

---

[297] *BOM*, 3 Nephi 21:14.

[298] *See BOM*, 3 Nephi, chapters 12, 13, and 14. *See also PGP*, JSH 1:34; *BOM*, Introduction.

[299] *BOM*, 3 Nephi 20:15.

[300] Matthew, chapters 5, 6, and 7.

[301] *BOM*, 3 Nephi, chapters 12, 13, and 14.

and all their enemies shall be cut off. Yea, wo be unto the Gentiles except they repent. ...

And I say unto you, that if the Gentiles do not repent after the blessing which they shall receive, after they have scattered my people—Then shall ye, who are a remnant of the house of Jacob, go forth among them; and ye shall be in the midst of them who shall be many; and ye shall be among them as a lion among the beasts of the forest, and as a young lion among the flocks of sheep, who, if he goeth through both treadeth down and teareth in pieces, and none can deliver.[302]

No weapon is quite like a nuclear weapon at "tear[ing a person] in pieces." Who is delivered (saved) during a nuclear explosion?[303]

---

[302] *BOM*, 3 Nephi 21:12–14; 20:15–17;

[303] "Nuclear explosion," *Wikipedia, The Free Encyclopedia*, last modified March 28, 2020, https://en.wikipedia.org/wiki/Nuclear_explosion; *see also* "Nuclear and radiation accidents and incidents," *Wikipedia, The Free Encyclopedia*, last modified March 18, 2020, https://en.wikipedia.org/wiki/Nuclear_and_radiation_accidents_and_incidents; *see also* "Chernobyl Accident 1986," *World Nuclear Association*, last modified March 2020,

In prophesying about what is about to happen in this world, we made it clear that "the power of God"[304] is soon to be with the poor and the needy, the sick and the afflicted, the tired, the downtrodden, the huddled masses, and the wretched refuse;[305] and that the "wrath of God"[306] will be upon all those who afflict them.[307]

Unless the United States of America begins to use its great power and influence to create equity upon Earth, using the "power of God"[308] for the intent to do good—to clothe the naked, and to feed the hungry, and to liberate the captive [as *they* were liberated], and administer relief to the sick and the afflicted,[309] domestic and foreign terrorism, using nuclear weapons, will destroy society ... just like it did in the ancient city of Atacama.[310]

---

https://www.world-nuclear.org/information-library/safety-and-security/safety-of-plants/chernobyl-accident.aspx.

[304] *BOM*, 1 Nephi 13:18–19, 30.

[305] "The New Colossus," https://en.wikipedia.org/wiki/The_New_Colossus.

[306] *BOM*, 1 Nephi 22:16.

[307] *THOR*, 315–18.

[308] *BOM*, 1 Nephi 13:18–19, 30.

[309] *BOM*, Jacob 2:19.

[310] *See* pages 106–8 in this book to refer back to Atacama.

The United States of America is the *only* country who has the power and ability to spearhead (initiate and lead) this "intent to do good."[311]

We know this in the same way that we knew that the United States of America would become "another beast coming up out of the earth" to replace the "first beast"[312] unto which "the dragon gave power, and his seat, and great authority."[313]

The first beast we referred to in our book of Revelation was the Great Roman Empire.[314] We referred to the Eastern Empire as "one of his heads as it were wounded to death; and his deadly wound was healed; and all the world wondered after the beast."[315]

At the time we wrote Revelation, the Western Empire of the Great Roman Empire was one of the "heads" and the Eastern Empire was the other. The Eastern Empire "was

---

[311] *BOM*, Jacob 2:19.

[312] *See 666 America*, 293–316, especially 302–7.

[313] *See* Revelation 13:1–12.

[314] *666 America*, 297–8.

[315] Revelation 13:3. *666 America*, 296–8.

healed" and became the Roman Catholic Church, to which "all the world wondered after."[316]

We knew that eventually

another beast [would come] up out of the earth; and he had two horns like a lamb, and he spake as a dragon ... And he doeth great wonders, so that he maketh fire come down from heaven on the earth in the sight of men.[317]

This was our reference at the time to the power of nuclear energy.

We knew that this second beast would "deceive them that dwell on the earth by the means of the miracles which he had power to do in the sight of the beast"[318] ("miracles" are referring to the great technological and industrial advancements.) These *miracles* would cause all people

---

[316] Revelation 13:3.

[317] Revelation 13:11, 13. *See also 666 America*, 308–9.

[318] Revelation 13:14.

that dwell on the earth to "give life to and worship the image of the beast."[319]

We knew that the same "dragon"[320] that gave the Great Roman Empire its "power, seat, and authority"[321] would one day give the United States the same. America would become "another beast coming up out of the earth"[322] to replace the first "beast" unto which "the dragon gave ... power, and his seat, and great authority."[323]

In 2006, we published a complete unfolding of our book of Revelation, titled *666, the Mark of America, Seat of the Beast—The Apostle John's New Testament Revelation Unfolded*.[324] We did this to fulfill our new American scripture's prophecies.[325] This book presents the concepts that we intended along the lines of accepted Christian belief: the Second Coming of Jesus Christ.[326]

---

[319] Revelation 13:13–15.

[320] Revelation 13:2, 4. *See also 666 America*, 5–8, 16, 275, and 292.

[321] Revelation 13:2.

[322] Revelation 13:11.

[323] Revelation 13:2.

[324] *666 America*, https://www.realilluminati.org/666-mark-of-america.

[325] *BOM*, 1 Nephi 14:18–28.

[326] *See* pages 159–62 of this book concerning the "Second Coming."

After we presented what the United States had become by the time we published our book in 1830, we included a way to explain what we knew was going to happen in the future to this "second beast,"[327] IF the Gentiles rejected our message.[328]

Our character, Nephi, sees the rise and establishment of the United States of America in vision.[329] It would be easy for a critic to say that Joseph Smith made up that vision according to what had already taken place in America by the early 19th century. But what any critic *cannot* explain is why we included the importance of the book of Revelation in our narrative. (We will explain below.)

Joseph Smith *did* explain to his followers about the "power and dominion of the god of this world."[330] This *devil* would influence and support the Industrial Revolution that was about to take place *after* 1830, which would affect the entire world. In 1831, Joseph Smith gave a revelation "from

---

[327] *See 666 America*, 302–5.
[328] *See BOM*, 1 Nephi 14:19–28, *especially* vs. 24–6.
[329] *See BOM*, 1 Nephi, chapters 12–14.
[330] *See BOM*, Mosiah 3:19 concerning the "natural man." *See also SNS*, 87–8, where *Lucifer* answers Adam's prayer. *See also 666 America*, 308–11.

the Lord"[331] that explains clearly that the devil *did not yet* have full power and control over the world.

"The Lord" explained:

And again, verily I say unto you, O inhabitants of the earth: I the Lord am willing to make these things known unto all flesh; For I am no respecter of persons, and will that all men shall know that the day speedily cometh; the hour is not yet [1831], but is nigh at hand, when peace shall be taken from the earth, and the devil shall have power over his own dominion.[332]

The Industrial Revolution[333] started earlier in American history, before 1831, but it did not reach the pinnacle of its "power [and] dominion" until well after Joseph gave his followers this revelation.

---

[331] *JS Bio*, "Joseph's 'Revelations,'" 328–9.

[332] *D&C*, 1:34–5.

[333] "Industrial Revolution," *Wikipedia, The Free Encyclopedia*, last modified April 6, 2020, https://en.wikipedia.org/wiki/Industrial_Revolution.

This "power over his [the devil's] own dominion"[334] is what we referred to in Revelation as "those miracles which [America] had power to do," and to which all people on Earth "make an image."[335]

Nothing has been more powerful over the hearts and minds of the people on Earth than the image of the *American Dream.*[336]

We had the angel in Nephi's vision tell him that

the things which thou shalt see hereafter [after 1830] thou shalt not write; for the Lord God hath ordained the apostle of the Lamb of God that he should write them.[337]

Here was our first introduction to our book of Revelation's narrative about "the end of the world":

---

[334] *See D&C*, 1:35.
[335] *See* Revelation 13:14; *see also 666 America*, 308–11.
[336] *See 666 America*, 295, 310, 366, and Index: "American Dream."
   See also "American Dream," *Wikipedia, The Free Encyclopedia*, last modified March 15, 2020, https://en.wikipedia.org/wiki/American_Dream.
[337] *BOM*, 1 Nephi 14:25.

Behold, he [the apostle of the Lamb of God (John)] shall see and write the remainder of these things; yea, and also many things which have been. And [the author of Revelation] shall also write concerning the end of the world. ... But the things which thou shalt see hereafter thou shalt not write; for the Lord God hath ordained the apostle of the Lamb of God that he should write them.[338]

This is the point when we also included an introduction to the "sealed portion," or the "greater portion" of our new American scripture:

And also others who have been, to them hath he shown all things, and they have written them; and they are sealed up to come forth in their purity.[339]

By the end of our story, we included the importance of our "sealed portion" and, again, the importance of the book

---

[338] *BOM*, 1 Nephi 14:21–2, 25.
[339] *BOM*, 1 Nephi 14:26.

of Revelation. We explained that when *The Sealed Portion — The Final Testament of Jesus Christ* was published to the world, Revelation would also be "unfolded in the eyes of all the people."[340] Not just in the eyes of the Mormons and the Christians, but in the eyes of <u>all</u> the people on Earth.

Our unfolding of Revelation's secret meaning, which only we knew, would announce the beginning of "the work of the Father,"[341] which is our work as the Real Illuminati™.

The complete unfolding of the meaning of Revelation offers empirical evidence of our existence and work. For hundreds of years, no one on Earth was able to decipher Revelation's true meaning. The book *666, the Mark of America, Seat of the Beast* unfolds its meaning.[342] The explanations given in that book are unchallengeable and have never been disputed, nor can they be.

The mention of the importance of Revelation in conjunction with the "sealed portion" of our new American scripture[343] is hard to ignore. But it has been ignored.

---

[340] *See BOM*, Ether 4:16.
[341] *BOM*, Ether 4:17.
[342] *666 America*, https://www.realilluminati.org/666-mark-of-america.
[343] *See BOM*, 1 Nephi 14:26 and *BOM*, Ether 4:16–17.

The American Gentiles have ignored our book. The church that proclaims belief in our book as another testament of Jesus Christ has transfigured our book and turned it into something that it is not.

Through *A New American Scripture—How and Why the Real Illuminati™ Created the Book of Mormon*, we are going to prove, unequivocally, indisputably, and clearly, that we, a group known today as the Real Illuminati™, created the *Book of Mormon*.

We created the presentation of *how* this first-of-its-kind, new American scripture came to be. We recruited Joseph Smith, Jr., a young American teenager, to help us. We instructed and guided him through the entire process.

We introduced ourselves to Joseph Smith, Jr. in September of 1823. Over four years, we prepared him for the task of assisting us in revealing our new American scripture. During this time, we prepared the means by which the book would be written. We made plates constructed of a metal alloy that had the appearance of gold. We gave Joseph the means by which he then transferred the meaning of the characters we engraved upon those plates into the English language.

Those plates became the source from which we conveyed the words of our new American scripture to the world, through Joseph Smith, Jr. We used those plates to prove to the world, through the empirical witness of three sworn affiants,[344] that the source of the new scripture was *not* Joseph.

In September of 1827, when we knew he was ready to fulfill the task, we allowed Joseph (who was then 21 years old) to announce to his family and friends that he had been chosen to bring forth our new American scripture. Over the next three years, three people acted as his scribes: Joseph's wife, Emma Hale Smith; his friend, Martin Harris; and a schoolteacher we recruited to help him, Oliver Cowdery.

We instructed Joseph on how to announce the book's existence. We instructed him on what *not* to say about our book. We instructed Joseph on every step in bringing our new scripture to the American people.

---

[344] *See BOM*, "Introduction, The Testimony of Three Witnesses" (Oliver Cowdery, David Whitmer, and Martin Harris).

Our book was intended for humans who had settled in the Western Hemisphere. Particularly, it was for the European Christians of the Protestant sects, who had immigrated to America from the Eastern Hemisphere and had brought the Bible and their Protestant forms of Christianity with them.

We could not introduce a new scripture, presenting it as another source of "God's word" consistent with the Bible, until the United States of America had been legally established and the freedoms of religion and speech were given protection under the law.

In *A New American Scripture—How and Why the Real Illuminati™ Created the Book of Mormon*, we will give the details of our involvement in getting the Bill of Rights (1791) amended to the original U.S. Constitution, which was originally adopted and ratified in 1788. Without these important amendments, which included the First Amendment right to freedom of religion, we would not have been able to introduce a new religious scripture authority (the *Book of Mormon*).

Along with exposing how our *Book of Mormon* has been misused by the Mormon faith, in *A New American Scripture—How and Why the Real Illuminati™ Created the Book of Mormon*, we will give more important details about our meetings with Thomas Jefferson and James Madison. We will explain how we influenced them to amend the U.S. Constitution with the Bill of Rights. We will share how we first met with them and introduced our idea of influencing a new religious movement.

We will explain in clear detail how and why we created a *new American scripture* in hopes of influencing righteous works by a nation "above all other nations."[345]

---

[345] *BOM*, 1 Nephi 13:30.

A New American Jesus

Part Three

An appropriate description of our (the Real Illuminati™'s) goals is:

> to oppose superstition, obscurantism, religious influence over public life, the abuses of state power and to put an end to the machinations of the purveyors of injustice, to control them without dominating them.[346]

Writing a new American scripture was one of the ways we determined was necessary to "control" early European-American Christians without impeding their free will ("without dominating them").

Religious influence, mainly of the Orthodox and Protestant Christian varieties, have held enormous influence over public life. The secret combination of

---

[346] "About Us—The Real Illuminati™," *Real Illuminati™*, accessed March 29, 2020, https://www.realilluminati.org/about-us.

religious, political, and business power and influence exists the same today as this *combination* did during the early history of the United States of America. This secret combination has led to great abuses of state power. It has caused division, "lyings and deceivings, whoredoms, secret abominations, idolatries, murders, and priestcrafts, envyings, strifes, and all manner of wickedness and abominations."[347]

To control them without dominating them, we needed to get people to believe in something that would counter abuses of power and what the combination of religious and political power does to public life.

We knew that people believed in Jesus Christ as *their* God and Savior. But we needed to get them to believe in *our* Jesus Christ. If we could get them to accept *our Savior* over theirs, we could control them by *our* word of God. To accomplish this, we gave them words from the mouth of *their* Savior, but delivered by the mouth of *ours*.

---

[347] *Compare BOM*, 3 Nephi 30:2.

Our new American scripture did not present a different Jesus than the one in which the Christians already believed. We used the same idea for our Jesus[348] as was presented to the early European-American Christians in the New Testament of the King James Bible.[349]

Our story's Jesus Christ used the exact same words that *their Savior* spoke while he was on Earth,[350] according to the New Testament. The words that we wanted to use to control the people were the words that were known throughout Christianity as the *Sermon on the Mount* (given in Matthew, chapters 5, 6, and 7).

We knew that the European-American Christians already had a strong belief in *their* Jesus Christ. Their faith and belief wouldn't exist without the New Testament stories of Jesus. We also knew that the New Testament stories would not, and could not, exist without the Old Testament stories. We incorporated both sets of stories into our new American scripture.[351]

---

[348] *BOM*, 3 Nephi, chapters 11–26, *see specifically* chapters 12, 13, and 14.
[349] Matthew, chapters 5, 6 and 7.
[350] *BOM*, 3 Nephi, chapters 12, 13, and 14.
[351] "Book of Mormon," https://www.realilluminati.org/the-book-of-mormon.

But there was a twist that we needed to use in order to plagiarize (copy) the Bible's story of Jesus and present it as our own.

To get them to consider that *their* Jesus was not being presented correctly by their corrupt Christian leaders, we needed to introduce a level of doubt in *their* accepted version of the Bible. We needed to impress upon the early American Christians that their version of the story of Jesus as presented in their Bible—the King James Version being the most prominent among them—was causing "an exceedingly great many [to] stumble, yea, insomuch that Satan hath great power over them."[352]

To do this, we began our story in Old Testament Jerusalem, 600 BCE. Our story begins with the introduction of a prominent Hebrew family living in Jerusalem shortly before the city was destroyed by the Babylonians. The family's patriarch is named Lehi.[353]

---

[352] *See BOM*, 1 Nephi 13:29.
[353] *BOM*, 1 Nephi 1:5.

Lehi was a very prominent and wealthy[354] High Priest in the Hebrew church. Two holy men (prophets) were sent to Jerusalem to call the people to repentance and warn of their sacred city's impending doom. Lehi was the only High Priest who believed the prophets. Distraught, Lehi went home and cried. He prayed "even with all his heart, in behalf of his people."[355]

While he prayed, Lehi saw a vision.[356] In the vision, he saw the future Jesus Christ and his twelve disciples teaching the people in Jerusalem, according to the story of the New Testament. This vision overwhelmingly convinced Lehi of the great importance of this future Jesus and his disciples.

Lehi tried to get the people to listen to the prophets' warnings.[357] The people refused and instead mocked him.[358] Lehi had four sons. The oldest was Laman; the next

---

[354] *BOM*, 1 Nephi 2:4, 11; 3:16, 22.
[355] *BOM*, 1 Nephi 1:5.
[356] *BOM*, 1 Nephi 1:8–15.
[357] *BOM*, 1 Nephi 1:18.
[358] *BOM*, 1 Nephi 1:19.

was Lemuel, then Nephi, and Sam.[359] Laman and Lemuel did not trust and believe their father[360]. Nephi and Sam did.[361]

Lehi's life was being threatened[362] because of what he was saying about the Hebrew church and about its leaders and the people: "Wo, wo, unto Jerusalem, for I have seen thine abominations!"[363]

In the first draft of our story, we detailed what these "abominations" were. These "abominations" were what the early European-American Christians were doing in *their* religious worship and doings. Those who read our first draft were greatly offended by our condemnation of all organized religion. Consequently, we were forced to rewrite the first part of our story's plot.

In rewriting our story's plot, we needed to maintain a consistent flow among the characters, as we had presented them in our original story about Lehi. Realizing that potential

[359] *BOM*, 1 Nephi 2:5.
[360] *BOM*, 1 Nephi 2:12–13.
[361] *BOM*, 1 Nephi 2:16–17.
[362] *BOM*, 1 Nephi 1:20.
[363] *BOM*, 1 Nephi 1:13.

critics now had access to our original manuscript, we needed a short time to rewrite the story so that it would flow well.

To gain some time to rework our story, we counseled Joseph to allow his scribe, Martin Harris, to show the 116 pages of handwritten manuscript to those in his family and of his friends who were critical of his involvement in writing the book. This was *after* Joseph had read the manuscript to those who believed in what he was doing—who were an unsuspecting peer review group of our writings. As we have explained, those who believed that Joseph was telling them the truth about our book had a hard time with the implication of the abomination of *all* organized religion.

If those *closest* to Joseph had a hard time accepting the new ideas we were presenting about religion, it became obvious to us that few others would have any desire to continue reading a book that they, as a Christian reader, might feel was anti-religious.

Therefore, we allowed Joseph to turn over the 116-page manuscript[364] to his critics (Martin Harris' family and friends).[365] We knew that it was a possibility that the original manuscript would be "lost" (stolen). We expected it. We knew that our enemies might use the original manuscript to discredit Joseph's claims of divine authorship from characters engraved on metal plates.

But unlike the distorted and slanted history given by Brigham Young's Utah church,[366] we knew what the possibilities were when *we allowed* Joseph to let Harris take the manuscript home.

Modern Mormons are led to believe that Joseph made a mistake in letting Harris take the manuscript. If Joseph was "called of God," and Joseph was a prophet, seer, and revelator of God's will, how could it have been possible that God didn't know what was going to happen? Does God make mistakes?

---

[364] *See TSP*, "Book of Lehi," 599–633.

[365] *D&C*, sections 3 and 10.

[366] "Lost Manuscript of the Book of Mormon," *The Church of Jesus Christ of Latter-day Saints*, accessed April 5, 2020, https://www.churchofjesuschrist.org/study/history/topics/lost-manuscript-of-the-book-of-mormon.

When faced with this obvious reflection, Mormons are convinced that Joseph made an error in his own judgment, against God's will. So the questions could be asked, "Was Joseph more powerful than God? Couldn't God have stopped him from doing what God didn't want him to do?"

Many modern LDS/Mormons claim that those who had the manuscript in their possession could have modified it. If that was possible, the modification of the words on the original paper on which the story was written would have been blatantly obvious. The confusion comes because the Mormons do *not* have the proper understanding of *how* the book was written and from what source it *really* came.

Although Mormons will say that they believe in the existence of the "Three Nephites" and "John the Beloved," as living mortals who do not age, get sick, or die,[367] they have no clue, nor can Mormons explain, what these immortal mortals are currently doing with their time.

We explained our existence (the Real Illuminati™) in our book's storyline. We gave strong clues about what we

---

[367] *See BOM*, 3 Nephi, chapter 28.

were and are doing "among the Gentiles."[368] We wrote our own introduction in the *Book of Mormon* to compliment and give clue of our involvement with Joseph Smith.

"Mormon" is the character in our story who is writing the *Book of Mormon*. As Mormon writes his story about *our* Jesus, he "[sees us], and they have ministered unto me."[369]

We then presented clues about what we would do in the future:

And behold they will be among the [Americans], and the Gentiles shall know them not. They will also be among the Jews, and the Jews shall know them not.

And it shall come to pass, when the Lord seeth fit in his wisdom that they shall minister unto all the scattered tribes of Israel, and unto all nations, kindreds, tongues and people, and shall bring out of them unto Jesus many souls, that their desire

---

[368] *See BOM*, 3 Nephi, chapter 28.
[369] *BOM*, 3 Nephi 28:26.

may be fulfilled, and also because of the convincing power of God which is in them.

And they are as the angels of God, and if they shall pray unto the Father in the name of Jesus they can show themselves unto whatsoever man it seemeth them good.

THEREFORE, great and marvelous works shall be wrought by them, before the great and coming day when all people must surely stand before the judgment-seat of Christ; Yea even among the Gentiles shall there be a great and marvelous work wrought by them, before that judgment day.[370]

The modern LDS/Mormons incorrectly assume that their religion, their faith, and their organization is the "great and marvelous work"[371] promised in our new American scripture.

---

[370] *BOM*, 3 Nephi 28:27–32, emphasis added.
[371] *See BOM*, 3 Nephi 28:31.

If so, then accordingly and appropriately, WE (the Real Illuminati™) would be running the Church of Jesus Christ of Latter-day Saints. On the contrary, we have nothing to do with that corrupt religion.

Since Brigham Young took over the reins of mainstream Mormonism, not one leader, not one ... not even a single one ... has ever mentioned us or our existence, and certainly not anything about *our* "great and marvelous work."[372]

The clues about the work that we would do among the Americans (Gentiles) couldn't have been stated any clearer. WE are the "them" by which these "great and marvelous works shall be wrought."[373]

It wasn't an angel that led the young American teenager to dig up gold plates. WE did.[374]

WE constructed the metal plates—with the appearance of gold. WE dug a hole and included a few other ancient artifacts and the means that would influence and

---

[372] *BOM*, 3 Nephi 28:31.

[373] *BOM*, 3 Nephi 28:31.

[374] *See PGP*, JSH 1:34–54.

convince an American teenager to help us write our book, while we worked with him behind the scenes.

Accordingly, and for the same desires and purpose, WE led a few young Bedouin shepherd boys (in 1947) to discover the caverns[375] in which WE had hidden the Dead Sea Scrolls many years before.

Why did we write and hide what the world knows as the Dead Sea Scrolls?[376]

Keep in mind that our new American scripture was meant for European-American Christians. We wrote this new scripture to introduce a different way of looking at Jesus and what his work was, as we have explained above.

After the Roman Catholic Church introduced *its* version of Jesus, and canonized *their version*, many religions developed from this inaccurate perception. The Catholic (Greek, meaning *global*) Jesus and Christianity was being used to control the masses and enrich the few. To

---

[375] "The Leon Levy Dead Sea Scrolls Digital Library | Discovery and Publication," *Israel Antiquities Authority*, accessed April 6, 2020, https://www.deadseascrolls.org.il/learn-about-the-scrolls/discovery-and-publication?locale=en_US.

[376] "Dead Sea Scrolls," *Wikipedia, The Free Encyclopedia*, last modified March 29, 2020, https://en.wikipedia.org/wiki/Dead_Sea_Scrolls.

counter this, we set up empirical evidence that we would allow to later be discovered that would cause an honest person to doubt and question the Catholic perception of Jesus and his work.

The Dead Sea Scrolls, if studied honestly and openly, present the idea of a "Teacher of Righteousness,"[377] who taught and did some of the same things that the Catholic Jesus supposedly did. But it can be proven, empirically and historically, that this "teacher of righteousness"[378] existed long before the Catholic Jesus Christ did.

We knew that the concept, myth, and legend that eventually created the Catholic Jesus was actually based on the life of a True Messenger whom we influenced during the 1st century *before Christ.*[379]

---

[377] *See THOR* (large print), 78. *See also* A. Dupont-Sommer, *The Dead Sea Scrolls* (Oxford: Basil Blackwell, 1952) 99, *which says*, "The Galilean Master, as He is presented to us in the writings of the New Testament, appears in many respects as an astonishing reincarnation of the Teacher of Righteousness"; *and* Fred Gladstone Bratton, *A History of the Bible* (Boston: Beacon Press, 1967) 79–80, *which says*, "The Teacher of Righteousness of the Scrolls would seem to be a prototype of Jesus."

[378] "Teacher of Righteousness," *Wikipedia, The Free Encyclopedia*, last modified January 31, 2020, https://en.wikipedia.org/wiki/Teacher_of_Righteousness.

[379] *THOR* (large print), 124–9.

Our "great and marvelous work"[380] is about trying to get people to accept *our Jesus* over the one presented by the Catholic religion. The *Catholic Jesus* influenced the Jesus in which all the other Protestant and breakaway Christian sects believe, including ALL of the early American Christian faiths.

We were trying to control them without dominating them.

According to our story, ONLY OUR JESUS is the correct Jesus. ONLY OUR WORK is a work that can save humanity. This is why it is referred to as "a great and marvelous work wrought by [us], before that judgment day."[381]

This "judgment day" is meant to reflect the Christian belief of the Second Coming of Christ. However, modern Christians, including the deceived LDS/Mormons (who should know better), reject the idea that the Second Coming of Christ ALREADY OCCURRED.

Jesus came the *first* time to teach the Jews. As we intended to present in our storyline, Jesus came a SECOND

[380] *BOM*, 3 Nephi 28:31.
[381] *BOM*, 3 Nephi 28:31–2.

time to teach the ancient ancestors of the native Americans, both in the Western Hemisphere and upon the isles of the sea.[382]

Christians are taught by their corrupt leaders that Jesus Christ will one day return to the world and make things right. They are taught that the "wicked" people will be destroyed before the Second Coming. To keep our new American scripture's storyline consistent with orthodox Christian beliefs, the entire Great Nation that consisted of Nephite and Lamanite peoples was destroyed before *our Second Coming* of *our* Jesus.

According to our presentation of *our* Jesus, millions of ancient American people (men, women, children, and infants) were burned, buried alive, drowned, and carried away by whirlwinds before *our Jesus's Second Coming*.

We needed to include the destruction of everyone, because this is what Christians believe that *their Jesus* is going to do before he comes again. It was our intent to present this *Second Coming* as it would occur *if* it actually

---

[382] *BOM*, 3 Nephi, chapter 11. *See also BOM*, 3 Nephi 16:1–3; *BOM*, 2 Nephi 29:7.

took place in the future, as orthodox Christians believe(d) that it would.

We knew that there would be no Second Coming of Jesus, because the Jesus in which the Christians believe is not real. Christians are controlled by their religious leaders—for the gain of these leaders—to believe that nothing can be done to help humanity until Jesus comes again. Until Jesus comes again, the people were and are dependent on their religious leaders to continue to prepare them for a *Second Coming*, which we presented has already taken place. Without their religious leaders, believers are convinced that they cannot do anything to change the world, because God only talks to His leaders.[383]

We had this second appearance take place to imply what *our Jesus*—the TRUE Jesus—would do *if* he came again.

---

[383] Russell M. Nelson, "Sustaining the Prophets," *The Church of Jesus Christ of Latter-day Saints*, October 5, 2014, https://www.churchofjesuschrist.org/study/general-conference/2014/10/sustaining-the-prophets, "The Lord's voice … comes through the voice of His servants, the prophets."

Henry B. Eyring, "The Lord Leads His Church," *The Church of Jesus Christ of Latter-day Saints*, September 30, 2017, https://www.churchofjesuschrist.org/study/general-conference/2017/10/the-lord-leads-his-church, "[Jesus Christ] leads His Church today by speaking to men called as prophets, and He does it through revelation."

Mark E. Petersen, "Follow the Prophets," *The Church of Jesus Christ of Latter-day Saints*, October 4, 1981, https://www.churchofjesuschrist.org/study/general-conference/1981/10/follow-the-prophets, "God speaks through our great leaders and guides his people by their words."

Our *Second Coming of Christ* presented Jesus, the Christ, teaching the people what they needed to do to save humanity. He did not save the people, but taught them what needed to be done to save THEMSELVES.

Even if the corrupt idea of Jesus coming to Earth to save humanity *were* true, how does one suppose that Jesus is going to do it? Kill all the wicked first, then FORCE everyone else to do what he says?

What would it be that Jesus would say during his Second Coming?

Would he not deliver unto the people of the 21st century the same commandments and counsel he gave the people of the 1st century?

If it was the "fulness of the everlasting Gospel,"[384] then what Jesus told the Jews, and then the ancient native Americans, would be the same things that he would tell the Gentiles of the 21st century ... at least this is what we were trying to present and imply in our story.

---

[384] *See PGP*, JSH 1:34.

It was our desire to help Christians understand that *they* have the responsibility to do good and set up:

Zion (the New Jerusalem) ... built upon the American continent; [so] that Christ [can] reign personally upon the earth; and that the earth will be RENEWED and receive its paradisiacal glory.[385]

"Renewed" to what condition?

It does not say *save* or *change* the earth. It says, "the earth will be renewed." This means *renewed* to how it was *before* the "fall" of humankind, how we hoped people would imagine the environment that existed in the figurative "Garden of Eden."[386]

We knew that to do this, one cannot expect it to be done except by the free-willed actions of the people living on Earth. No human can be forced to do anything.

Sure, the false Christ *can* destroy someone who does not do the "right thing" ... just like *our Jesus* did to the

---

[385] *See PGP*, Articles of Faith 1:10, emphasis added.
[386] *See SNS*, 37–8, 41, 63–5. *See also JS Bio*, 108–9, 246–9.

ancient native Americans. This is what the Christians believed to whom we directed our new American scripture. If we had not presented a vindictive, angry, destroying Christ as coming a second time, the Christians wouldn't have accepted *our Jesus*.

It was our intent to counter the erroneous doctrine about the orthodox Jesus, the Christ. We knew that neither God nor Christ can solve humanity's problems. Humans must solve their own problems through "repentance"—realizing that their problems are wrong, stop doing what causes the problems, and never do them again.

To help prepare the people on Earth and to teach them what they need to do "*before* the great and coming day when all people must surely stand before the judgment-seat of Christ," we have been involved in "a great and marvelous work."[387]

"The judgment-seat of Christ" represents the time when all Christians must consider their works and be judged by what Christ told them to do when he was among them.

---

[387] *See BOM*, 3 Nephi 28:31.

In all of our efforts, we have had to confront the orthodox, Catholic-inspired, erroneous Jesus, who Christians believe, not only died for their sins, but also will come again and save them.

To counter them, to control them without dominating them, we simply direct Christians to ACTUALLY READ AND LISTEN TO JESUS' WORDS ... NONE OF WHICH support a person being forgiven of their sins *because* he was murdered after his simple message of salvation was rejected.

What was Jesus' message of salvation?

What was "the work" that "the only true God" sent Jesus Christ to do?

What was "the work" Jesus was referring to when, praying to God, he said, "I have finished the work which thou gavest me to do"?[388]

According to the stories accepted by orthodox Christianity, Jesus was alive and well when he prayed to his Father. Whatever it was the Father wanted the Son to do, Jesus FINISHED IT *before* he was murdered ... hung on a tree.

---

[388] John 17:4.

The work that the *true Jesus* was sent to Earth to do had nothing to do with Jesus being crucified on the cross. The same can be said of the Dead Sea Scrolls' "Teacher of Righteousness." He was also hung on a tree,[389] just like Jesus was: "The God of our fathers raised up Jesus, whom ye slew and hanged on a tree."[390]

The controversy over whether or not the Jesus spoken of in the New Testament was the same "teacher" mentioned in the Dead Sea Scrolls, has caused quite a stir[391] in the minds of scholars and scientists alike. We had hoped this would happen. This was the purpose for our producing and hiding the scrolls.

But the "great and marvelous work"[392] that *our Jesus* was going to do to save humanity was the main focus of our story.

---

[389] The Nahum Pesher from Cave 4 refers to "a man hanged alive on [the] tree," *in* Geza Vermes, *The Complete Dead Sea Scrolls in English (Revised Edition)* (London: Penguin Books, 2004), 505, https://epdf.pub/queue/the-complete-dead-sea-scrolls-in-english.html.

[390] Acts 5:30.

[391] *For one example, see* Edwin M. Yamauchi, "The Teacher of Righteousness from Qumran and Jesus of Nazareth," *Christianity Today* 10, no. 16 (May 13, 1966): 12, https://www.christianitytoday.com/ct/1966/may-13/teacher-of-righteousness-from-qumran-and-jesus-of-nazareth.html.

[392] *See BOM*, 3 Nephi 28:31.

Our work IS the:

great and marvelous works [that] shall be wrought by [us], before the great and coming day when all people must surely stand before the judgment-seat of Christ; Yea even among the Gentiles shall there be a great and marvelous work wrought by [us], before that judgment day.[393]

The "judgment day" to which we refer, and for which we exist to prepare the Americans (Gentiles) ... "the judgment-seat of Christ" ... is explained clearly in the New Testament as the time, "When the Son of man shall come in his glory, and all the holy angels with him, then shall he sit upon the throne of his glory."[394]

This prophecy, given from the mouth of Jesus himself, does NOT explain that he will straighten out the world and make it right! He sits in his "judgment seat" to judge the world.

---

[393] *BOM*, 3 Nephi 28:31–2.
[394] Matthew 25:31.

The GREAT JUDGMENT OF <u>OUR</u> JESUS CHRIST is based solely, ONLY, on one criterion (measure). This criterion has nothing to do with whether or not you have accepted Jesus Christ as your Lord and Savior. You can accept him all you want, but this acceptance, faith, and belief will not relieve you of his judgment when he comes in his glory!

Belonging to a church, being baptized, receiving all possible priesthood blessings and ordinance work, faithfully paying tithes and offerings, doing everything that your religious leaders have asked you to do ... in spite of all these many "righteous works"[395] ... when you stand in front of Jesus and his holy angels, he will only have a couple of questions to ask you:

Did you feed the least among you when they were hungry? Did you give water to the least among you, living in the arid parts of the world? Did you go there and dig wells from which they could

---

[395] *BOM*, Alma 5:17.

drink? The strangers who are at your borders trying to enter your country for food, shelter, clothing, healthcare, and education ... did you take these in? Did you clothe the naked? Did you support free and universal healthcare for the sick and least among you who cannot afford health insurance? Did you visit those in prison and treat them kindly as I would?[396]

Perhaps you will try to deflect Jesus' final judgment of you by saying,

Lord, Lord, have we not prophesied in thy name, and in thy name have cast out devils, and in thy name done many wonderful works?[397]

Perhaps you will be content with yourself, believing that although you were a miserable sinner during your life and treated others terribly, you have relied on the mercy

---

[396] *Compare* Matthew 25:31–6.
[397] *BOM*, 3 Nephi 14:22; Matthew 7:22.

of the false Jesus that you believed died for your sins to justify your actions?

Perhaps you will believe that "the genealogy of [your] fathers" is an important part that is "pleasing unto God and unto those who are not of the world."[398] But we have clearly explained that it is NOT! We have unmistakably explained that **ALL** genealogy work of any kind is "not of worth unto the children of men."[399]

So, when you are placed in front of and are being judged by the *real* "Son of man ... and all the holy angels with him, [as] he sit[s] upon the throne of his glory,"[400] perhaps you'll bring with you your completed genealogy work. Perhaps you'll bring your baptismal certificate, your tithing and donation receipts,[401] or maybe you'll bring your Temple

---

[398] *BOM*, 1 Nephi 6:1, 5. *See also* "Genealogy," *Church of Jesus Christ of Latter-day Saints*, accessed March 29, 2020, https://newsroom.churchofjesuschrist.org/topic/genealogy.

[399] *BOM*, 1 Nephi 6:1–6.

[400] Matthew 25:31.

[401] "Church Introduces Simplified Tithing, Donations Recording System," *The Church of Jesus Christ of Latter-day Saints*, accessed March 31, 2020, https://www.churchofjesuschrist.org/study/ensign/1982/01/news-of-the-church/church-introduces-simplified-tithing-donations-recording-system.

Recommend,[402] proving that you were a faithful follower and believer in Christ. But none of this is what the *real* Son of man considers, as you are judged and then directed to join those people whom he has "set on his left."[403]

In our *new American scripture*, we present the exact same teachings of Jesus. What he taught to the Jews is exactly what the *resurrected* Jesus taught the ancient inhabitants of the American continent.[404] Jesus taught the people things that they needed to know and do in order to change the course of human nature and save humanity. And about this, Jesus said:

> Therefore whosoever heareth these sayings of mine [what Jesus said in Matthew 5, 6, and 7 and repeated again in the *Book of Mormon*, 3 Nephi 12, 13, and 14], and doeth them, I will liken him unto a wise man, [who] built his house upon a rock. And

---

[402] Howard W. Hunter, "Your Temple Recommend," *The Church of Jesus Christ of Latter-day Saints*, accessed March 31, 2020, https://www.churchofjesuschrist.org/study/new-era/1995/04/your-temple-recommend.

[403] *See* Matthew 25:33.

[404] *See JS Bio*, 11–12, 292.

the rain descended, and the floods came, and the winds blew, and beat upon that house; and it fell not: for it was founded upon a rock.

And every one that heareth these sayings of mine, and doeth them not [that they did not do that which Jesus told the people to do in Matthew 5, 6, and 7 and again repeated in *BOM*, 3 Nephi 12, 13, and 14], shall be likened unto a foolish man, [who] built his house upon the sand: And the rain descended, and the floods came, and the winds blew, and beat upon that house; and it fell: and great was the fall of it.[405]

The "great and marvelous work"[406] that we have been trying to do among the American people, which commenced with writing our original manuscript for our story, has always been centered on saving humanity the

---

[405] Matthew 7:24–7.
[406] *BOM*, 3 Nephi 28:32.

only way it can be saved: by providing the basic necessities of life to all people on Earth fairly and impartially.

Our original manuscript (known as the lost 116-page manuscript)[407] prepared the reader for *our Jesus' Second Coming*, by having ancient prophets condemn the religion that the Hebrews had established, which included the Law of Moses and all of its rituals, ordinances, and what Isaiah referred to as "vain oblations."[408]

In our original draft, the prophets Zenos and Zenock were the ones who confronted the Hebrew church and its leaders. What our story's character, Lehi, heard them say was recorded in our original story.

As we explained and continue to reiterate, because the "abominations" that Zenos and Zenock called out[409] were parallel to the early American Christian churches' faith, doctrine, and works, Joseph Smith's (unknowing) *Peer Review Group* had a hard time with the comparison. The

---

[407] *See TSP*, "Book of Lehi," 591.
[408] Isaiah 1:13; *See also TSP*, Appendix 2, Lehi 1:31.
[409] *See TSP*, Lehi 1:46–2:45.

early American Christians could not imagine that their religion was so corrupt and an "abomination before God."

In our revised story, Lehi's two older sons also couldn't accept:

> [T]hat the people who were in the land of Jerusalem were [**not**] a righteous people; for they kept the statutes and judgments of the Lord, and all his commandments, according to the law of Moses; wherefore, [Laman and Lemuel believed] that they [*were*] a righteous people.[410]

Ironically, neither can the latter-day (modern) LDS/Mormon people—those who believe in the *Book of Mormon*—accept that they and their church and leaders are an "abomination before God."[411]

Mormons defend themselves against this accusation in the same way that Lehi's older sons did.

---

[410] *BOM*, 1 Nephi 17:22.
[411] *See* Isaiah, chapter 1. *See also TSP*, Appendix 2, Lehi 2:49.

We know that we are a righteous people because we keep the statutes and judgments of the Lord, and all his commandments, according to the law that our leaders receive from God [i.e., the modern-day Law of Moses].[412]

But if the Mormons would read our original presentation of Lehi's story,[413] they would be a bit more reluctant to use the above defense and justification.

In our original book of Lehi, what the prophets said to the people of Jerusalem was stated very clearly:

And there were many prophets sent forth by the Lord to bring the people of Jerusalem unto repentance. And when these prophets were bound and set before the chief priests of the people they were chastised and commanded to

---

[412] *Compare BOM*, 1 Nephi 17:22.
[413] "The Book of Lehi," *Real Illuminati*™, accessed March 29, 2020, https://www.realilluminati.org/the-book-of-lehi.

recant their prophecies and their testimonies and their preachings against the people.

For behold, the prophets did truly testify of the iniquities of the church at Jerusalem. For the people of the church were corrupted by the examples of their leaders who had the priesthood of God but lacked the power thereof, which power can only be exercised through the Holy Spirit; and this Spirit can only be controlled upon the principles of righteousness of him who was anointed to this priesthood. For the leaders were rich and popular men among the people, and had set themselves up above the people, even unto the envying of their positions by the people. And the leaders chose other leaders who were also rich and popular men among them. And in this way, the leaders of the Jewish people assured that all men who were chosen to the Priesthood would be like unto themselves.

And the people justified their own wicked state because of the examples of their leaders. Nevertheless, the leaders did not think of themselves as wicked, but as men whom God had blessed with riches and wisdom. And since the people believed that their leaders were indeed men of God, they were deceived into believing that riches and power and worldly glory were blessings of God. And in this way did Satan deceive the leaders; and the leaders did deceive the people.

And because the leaders did not believe that they were wicked, they taught the people that God would not speak to the people unless He did so through the channels of the priesthood of Aaron, which was established for this purpose. And the leaders taught the people that no High Priest belonging to the order of Aaron would be allowed by God to deceive the people. And in this way the High Priests assured themselves that the people would not be swayed by a doctrine outside of the church at Jerusalem, nor by other preaching that was not approved by them.

And the leaders of the people taught them the sacraments and the offerings and the ordinances of the church, which was established among the people according to the laws of Moses and according to the traditions of the Jews.[414]

...

Oh ye wicked and perverse generation. Why have ye polluted and corrupted the holy church of God? Why have ye led this people in such a way that the wrath of God will soon visit them even unto their own destruction? Behold, I say unto you, that their blood will be required at your hands because of your example and the things that ye

---

[414] *TSP*, Lehi 1:18–22.

have taught them. Nevertheless, their sins will be their own and they will also suffer because of them. But ye shall also suffer with them because ye have set yourselves up as the mouthpiece of God and have lied unto them by telling them that the Lord will not allow you to mislead them.

Behold, ye know not the words of God, but speak vanity and foolishness unto this people. Ye have taught this people that they should worship the church and the ordinances and the traditions thereof, and yet they deny the Spirit of God that will only dwell with the children of men in righteousness.

Do ye not remember the words of the prophet, Isaiah? Ye have them before you, yet ye understand them not. Ye hear them, but ye do not hear their true meaning. Ye read them, but ye do not understand that which ye have read, but ye have changed the doctrine of God to conform to your own selfish interests and desires.

Behold, did not Isaiah say unto this church: Thus saith the Lord, To what purpose is the multitude of your sacrifices unto me? Saith the Lord: I am full of the burnt offerings of rams, and the fat of fed beasts; and I delight not in the blood of bullocks, or of lambs, or of he-goats.[415]

At this point in our original story about Lehi and his dealings with the ancient Jews, we interpolated Isaiah, chapter one[416] ("Behold, did not Isaiah say unto this church..."). The early American Christian churches were <u>all</u> an "abomination before God."[417]

---

[415] *TSP*, Lehi 1:18–22, 26–9.

[416] (Beginning with Isaiah 1:11). *See TSP*, Lehi 1:29–38.

[417] *See* Isaiah, chapter 1; *PGP*, JSH 1:19–20. *See also TSP*, Appendix 3, "The First Vision," chapter 1, verse 21: "Behold, the religions and churches of men have always been an abomination before God, for He despiseth them, because they put one man above his neighbor in the things which they believe."

They [wore] stiff necks and high heads; yea, and because of pride, and wickedness, and abominations, and whoredoms, they [had] all gone astray save it be a few, who [were] the humble followers of Christ; nevertheless, they [were] led, that in many instances they [did] err because they [were] taught by the precepts of men.[418]

The "precepts of men" that were misleading the Christians were what the Christian leaders were teaching the people out of the Bible. But how could we prove this? How could we explain that the stories about Jesus told in the Bible were being used to mislead the people?

When our original storyline was rejected (*The Book of Lehi*, the 116-page lost manuscript),[419] we needed a way to introduce the idea that the King James Version of the Bible was corrupt. This is how we did it:

---

[418] *BOM*, 2 Nephi 28:14; *see also PGP*, JSH 1:19–20.
[419] *TSP*, "Book of Lehi," 599–633.

We had Lehi's son, Nephi, pray to God for a testimony of what his father was saying about the Hebrew people, and also about the coming of Jesus and his disciples in the future.

For it came to pass after I [Nephi] had desired to know the things that my father had seen, and believing that the Lord was able to make them known unto me, as I sat pondering in mine heart I was caught away in the Spirit of the Lord, yea, into an exceedingly high mountain, which I never had before seen, and upon which I never had before set my foot.[420]

This vision gave Nephi an understanding about Jesus and introduced the importance of what Jesus would teach to the Jews when he would live among them in Jerusalem. Here we presented what Jesus would teach the Jews as "the rod of iron ... the word of God ... the love of God."[421]

---

[420] *BOM*, 1 Nephi 11:1.
[421] *BOM*, 1 Nephi 11:25.

In Nephi's vision, he saw the New Testament storyline about Jesus Christ and his twelve disciples to the end when Jesus "was lifted up upon the cross and slain for the sins of the world."[422]

Nephi was shown the destruction of Jerusalem, and the "land of promise,"[423] to where Lehi's family would be led: the Western Hemisphere. The vision would include a history that we invented for Lehi's family, making them the ancient ancestors of the native American people.

As we explained above, our story presents that after Jesus was killed in the Eastern Hemisphere, he resurrected and came to the Western Hemisphere and taught the people the same things that he taught the Jews.

Our new American scripture begins with the importance of Jesus teaching the people the "word of God."[424] It was our original intention to end the story with the resurrected Jesus teaching the ancient native Americans the

[422] *BOM*, 1 Nephi 11:33.
[423] *BOM*, 1 Nephi 12:1.
[424] *BOM*, 1 Nephi 11:25.

same as that which he had taught the Jews,[425] which we called the "fulness of the everlasting Gospel."[426]

Some way, somehow, we had to use a palatable (believable) justification for our new American scripture in which "the fulness of the everlasting Gospel was contained ... as delivered by the Savior to the ancient inhabitants."[427]

We could not replace the Bible, nor could we discount it. How could we control the minds of the Christians without dominating them (taking away their free will)? How could we introduce the importance of our new American scripture and have the Christians accept it as "Another Testimony of Jesus Christ" as the Mormons would hypocritically proclaim,[428] albeit a *correct* one?

The way that we decided to do it was to present the King James Version of the Bible as an inefficient and incomplete record of Jesus' works and teachings. Here's how we did it:

---

[425] *BOM*, 3 Nephi, chapters 12, 13, and 14.

[426] *PGP*, JSH 1:34.

[427] *PGP*, JSH 1:34.

[428] *BOM*, Title Page. *See also* n. 454 of this book.

In Nephi's vision, he sees the establishment of the United States of America.[429] We called these early European-American colonists, "the Gentiles [who] had gone [forth] out of captivity [and] were delivered by the power of God out of the hands of all other nations."[430]

> And I, Nephi, beheld that the Gentiles [early European-Americans] that had gone out of captivity were delivered by the power of God out of the hands of all other nations.
>
> And it came to pass that I, Nephi, beheld that they did prosper in the land; and I beheld a book, and it was carried forth among them.
>
> And the angel said unto me: Knowest thou the meaning of the book? And I said unto him: I know not.
>
> ...

---

[429] *BOM*, 1 Nephi, chapter 13.
[430] *BOM*, 1 Nephi 13:19.

The book that thou beholdest is a record of the Jews [*the Old and New Testaments of the popular King James Bible*], which contains the covenants of the Lord, which he hath made unto the house of Israel; and it also containeth many of the prophecies of the holy prophets; and it is a record like unto the engravings which are upon the plates of brass [*the copy of the Old Testament carried to the Western Hemisphere by Lehi's family*], save there are not so many; nevertheless, they contain the covenants of the Lord, which he hath made unto the house of Israel; wherefore, they are of great worth unto the Gentiles.

And the angel of the Lord said unto me: Thou hast beheld that the book proceeded forth from the mouth of a Jew; and when it proceeded forth from the mouth of a Jew it contained the fulness of the gospel of the Lord, of whom the twelve apostles bear record; and they bear record according to the truth which is in the Lamb of God. Wherefore, these things go forth from the Jews in purity unto the Gentiles, according to the truth which is in God.

And after they go forth by the hand of the twelve apostles of the Lamb, from the Jews unto the Gentiles [*referring to the New Testament gospels and the other New Testament books attributed to Jesus' original twelve disciples*], thou seest the formation of that great and abominable church, which is most abominable above all other churches; for behold, they have taken away from the gospel of the Lamb many parts which are plain and most precious; and also many covenants of the Lord have they taken away.

And all this have they done that they might pervert the right ways of the Lord, that they might blind the eyes and harden the hearts of the children of men.

Wherefore, thou seest that after the book [*the Bible*] hath gone forth through the hands of the great and abominable church, that there are many plain and precious things taken away from the book, which is the book of the Lamb of God.

And after these plain and precious things were taken away it goeth forth unto all the nations of the Gentiles; and after it goeth forth unto all the nations of the Gentiles, yea, even across the many waters which thou hast seen with the Gentiles which have gone forth out of captivity, thou seest—because of the many plain and precious things which have been taken out of the book, which were plain unto the understanding of the children of men, according to the plainness which is in the Lamb of God—because of these things which are taken away out of the gospel of the

Lamb, **an exceedingly great many do stumble, yea, insomuch that Satan hath great power over them**.

Nevertheless, thou beholdest that the Gentiles who have gone forth out of captivity, and have been lifted up by the power of God above all other nations, upon the face of the land which is choice above all other lands, which is the land that the Lord God hath covenanted with thy father that his seed should have for the land of their inheritance; wherefore, thou seest that the Lord God will not suffer that the Gentiles will utterly destroy the mixture of thy seed, which are among thy brethren. Neither will he suffer that the Gentiles shall destroy the seed of thy brethren.

Neither will the Lord God suffer that the Gentiles shall forever remain in that awful state of blindness, which thou beholdest they are in, because of the plain and most precious parts of the gospel of the Lamb which have been kept back by that abominable church, whose formation thou hast seen.[431]

Our new American scripture would explain "the plain and most precious parts of the gospel of the Lamb which have been kept back by that abominable church."[432] This explanation and presentation is now part of the "great and marvelous work"[433] that we have done and are doing among the Americans. This includes, but is not limited to, creating the metal plates, engraving them, and then hiding them in a hole so that we could lead a young American teenager to them. (In the same way, we would later lead a couple of young Bedouin shepherd boys to a cave.)[434]

The church that developed after we introduced our new American scripture has not only ignored "the fulness of the everlasting Gospel ... as delivered by the Savior to the

---

[431] *BOM*, 1 Nephi 13:19–32, emphasis added.
[432] *BOM*, 1 Nephi 13:32.
[433] *BOM*, 3 Nephi 28:31–2.
[434] "Dead Sea Scrolls Digital Library."

ancient inhabitants,"[435] but it has also "kept back"[436] this gospel, which has no part of this church's current doctrine, covenants, rituals, ordinances, or anything else that it teaches the world.

The modern Church of Jesus Christ of Latter-day Saints, one of the wealthiest religions on Earth,[437] personifies the idea that we presented in our book as the "great and abominable church,"[438] more than any other church on Earth. We have named it the most evil religious institution in the world because of the way that it treats and ignores our new American scripture, the *Book of Mormon*.

Because the early American Christians who previewed our story had rejected its premise, we were forced to restructure our book accordingly so that we could control them without dominating them. This initial reaction to our original storyline prompted us to deliver the following words to those who would receive our record:

---

[435] *PGP*, JSH 1:34.
[436] *BOM*, 1 Nephi 13:32.
[437] Stack, "LDS Church kept the lid on its $100B fund."
[438] *See BOM*, 1 Nephi, chapters 13–14.

Hearken, O ye Gentiles, and hear the words of Jesus Christ, the Son of the living God, which he hath commanded me that I should speak concerning you, for, behold he commandeth me that I should write, saying:

Turn, all ye Gentiles, from your wicked ways; and repent of your evil doings, of your lyings and deceivings, and of your whoredoms, and of your secret abominations, and your idolatries, and of your murders, and your priestcrafts,[439] and your envyings, and your strifes, and from all your wickedness and abominations, and come unto me, and be baptized in my name, that ye may receive a remission of your sins, and be filled with the Holy Ghost, that ye may be numbered with my people who are of the house of Israel.[440]

---

[439] Definition: "1. the art and skills involved in the work of a priest. 2. (*derogatory*) the influence of priests upon politics or the use by them of secular power." *See* "priestcraft" in *Collins English Dictionary*, accessed April 4, 2020, https://www.collinsdictionary.com/dictionary/english/priestcraft.

[440] *BOM*, 3 Nephi 30:1–2.

These words were the LAST WORDS that we had *our Jesus* tell the Americans. *Our Jesus* does not mention that he will come again to the world. *Our Jesus* "finished the work which [God gave him] to do."[441]

The only "great and marvelous work"[442] left to be done after this *Second Coming of Christ* to the ancient native Americans, is the work that we are doing today ... for the intent to do good.

The European-American Christians were given the chance to do the right thing. We presented them with all the information they needed to do the right thing, even to form the right religion, because they desired one, but only if their "intent [was] to do good."[443]

We gave them "Another Testament of Jesus Christ"[444] that contains the "fulness of the everlasting Gospel ... as delivered by the Savior to the ancient inhabitants."[445]

[441] *See* John 17:4.
[442] *See BOM*, 3 Nephi 28:31–2.
[443] *BOM*, Jacob 2:19.
[444] *BOM*, Title Page.
[445] *PGP*, JSH 1:34.

We took the words of Jesus from the New Testament and had the exact same words come out of the mouth of our *new American* Jesus. What was written in the New Testament, Matthew, chapters 5, 6, and 7, was inserted into our scripture as 3 Nephi 12, 13, and 14. This was the Sermon on the Mount. This was the "fulness," the "rod of iron," the "word of [the Son of] God."[446]

We structured our storyline to incorporate something that we hoped would help control the minds and hearts of the early European-American Christians, whom we called the Gentiles.

We did everything in our power to instill in their hearts a "hope in Christ."[447] But their pride was too strong. Their pride and egos did to *our Christ* what the Jew's pride did to *theirs* (as we presented it):

And I, Nephi, saw that he was lifted up upon the cross and slain for the sins of the world. And after he was slain I saw the multitudes of the earth, that

---

[446] *PGP*, JSH 1:34; *BOM*, 1 Nephi 11:25.
[447] *BOM*, Jacob 2:19.

they were gathered together to fight against the apostles of the Lamb; for thus were the twelve called by the angel of the Lord.

And the multitude of the earth was gathered together; and I beheld that they were in a large and spacious building, like unto the building which my father saw. And the angel of the Lord spake unto me again, saying: Behold the world and the wisdom thereof; yea, behold the house of Israel hath gathered together to fight against the twelve apostles of the Lamb.

And it came to pass that I saw and bear record, that the great and spacious building was the pride of the world.[448]

We explained that this "pride of the world" is what the character Lucifer represented in our 1842 play.[449]

---

[448] *BOM*, 1 Nephi 11:33–6.
[449] *Sacred, not Secret*, https://www.realilluminati.org/sacred-not-secret.

We structured our new American scripture to counter the pride of the American people, especially the pride we knew that the members of the LDS/Mormon Church (the most evil religion upon Earth, as we have explained)[450] would have:

O that he would show you that he can pierce you, and with one glance of his eye he can smite you to the dust! O that he would rid you from this iniquity and abomination [pride]. And, O that ye would listen unto the word of his commands, and let not this pride of your hearts destroy your souls!

Think of your brethren like unto yourselves, and be familiar with all and free with your substance, that they may be rich like unto you. But before ye seek for riches, seek ye for the kingdom of God.

And after ye have obtained a hope in Christ ye shall obtain riches, if ye seek them; and ye will seek them

---

[450] *See* specifically pages 56, 123–4, and 191 of this book.

for the intent to do good—to clothe the naked, and to feed the hungry, and to liberate the captive, and administer relief to the sick and the afflicted.[451]

We structured our new scripture so that it might control them without dominating them. We structured it to prepare the Christians for the final judgment of their Christ, when he comes in his glory to judge the world ... according to Jesus' words in Matthew, chapter 25.[452]

Our scripture failed to control them. We could not get them to fully accept *our* Jesus, because of the pride they had in theirs.

Wanting to be popular in the eyes of the world, LDS/Mormon missionaries do not point out that the King James Bible is a corrupt presentation of Jesus' teachings and covenants, as our new American scripture clearly states.

Mormons couldn't rename our new American scripture: *The Book of Mormon, The Plain and Precious Testament of Jesus Christ—A Fullness of Christ's*

---

[451] *BOM*, Jacob 2:15–19.
[452] Matthew 25:31–40.

Everlasting Gospel. They couldn't do this because they rejected *our Jesus.* Modern LDS/Mormon teachings support *their Jesus*, their own god, the world's Jesus, the early American Christian Jesus, the King James Bible's Jesus ... a corrupt Jesus.

This form of a "great and abominable church"[453] named it, "Another Testament of Jesus Christ,"[454] "insomuch that Satan hath great power over them."[455]

Lucifer, the god of this world, the pride of this world, controls them and dominates them. Because of this pride, they have created the wealthiest church on Earth ... truly a Great and Abominable Church!

---

[453] *See BOM,* 1 Nephi, chapters 13–14.

[454] This took place in 1982. *See* Paul C. Gutjahr, *Lives of Great Religious Books* (Princeton: Princeton Univ. Press, 2012), 110, https://books.google.com/books?id=Mmz4Eob3MDkC.

[455] *BOM,* 1 Nephi 13:29.

Plain and Precious Things

Part Four

When we wrote our new American scripture, we did not "disclose [our] true identity."[456] This means more than not disclosing our personal names or whereabouts. It was also meant, as Joseph Smith often told his followers, "If I told you all that I know about the mysteries of God, you would rise up and kill me."[457]

Joseph Smith did not "disclose [his] true identity"[458] to the people of his day who read our *Book of Mormon* and accepted our story as another part of God's word.

As we have explained numerous times throughout this introductory five-part presentation to our book, *A New American Scripture*, when we introduced the first scene (chapter) of our book, we instructed Joseph to allow it to be

---

[456] *See SNS*, 94–5, 98. *See also JS Bio*, 24–5 and Appendix 3, "Without Disclosing Their True Identity: Why True Messengers Do Not Reveal The Real Truth," 676–80.

[457] Joseph Smith, Jr., "Brethren, if I were to tell you all I know of the kingdom of God, I do know that you would rise up and kill me." Pratt, "Reminiscences," 585, https://contentdm.lib.byu.edu/digital/collection/MStar/id/19227/rec/55.

[458] *See SNS*, 95–8.

peer reviewed so that we could determine if our storyline's message was well received and understood. The American Christians rejected it because of its clear message of the corrupt nature of ANY religious group or movement. They wanted a new religion, one based on their pride and ego (*Lucifer*). Therefore, we were forced to change the first chapter of our book (the chapter of Lehi, otherwise known as the 116-page manuscript).

We preserved our book's narrative, but in order for it to be accepted and read, we had to remove any indication that religion was corrupt and evil.[459]

In our reworked presentation of the *Book of Mormon* narrative, we made it clear what we were doing. We desired that the American Christians would read our new American scripture and apply it to their own situation. But we failed to convince them of anything that didn't support their own pride and ego ... the devil that held them captive in chains.

---

[459] *See TSP*, "Book of Lehi," *starting on page* 591.

Regardless, in our revised storyline, we explained the counsel that we gave to our messenger:

But behold, the Jews [American Christians] were a stiffnecked [prideful] people; and they despised the words of plainness [as we had presented them in our first, original chapter], and killed the prophets [would have killed Joseph], and sought for things that they could not understand. Wherefore, because of their blindness, which blindness came by looking beyond the mark[460] [the target that our book was written in the first place to hit—the *mark* it was meant to leave on society], they must needs fall; for God hath taken away his plainness from them, and delivered unto them many things which they cannot understand, because they desired it. And because they desired it God hath done it, that they may stumble.[461]

---

[460] *See also TSP*, 36:55; *THOR* (large print), 301–2, 315; *JS Bio*, 210.
[461] *Compare BOM*, Jacob 4:14.

Per capita, modern LDS/Mormons use more prescription medication for depression than any other group of humans on Earth.[462] They have fulfilled and are fulfilling the prophecies we established in the storyline for our new American scripture:

> For the time cometh, saith the Lamb of God, that I will work a great and a marvelous work among the children of men; a work which shall be everlasting, either on the one hand or on the other—either to the convincing of them unto peace and life eternal, or unto the deliverance of them to the hardness of their hearts and the blindness of their minds unto their being brought down into captivity, and also into destruction, both temporally and spiritually, according to the captivity of the devil, of which I have spoken.[463]

---

[462] Goldman, "Two Studies."
[463] *BOM*, 1 Nephi 14:7.

Temporally (in regards to money and material possessions), the LDS/Mormon Church is one of the wealthiest religions in the world[464] ... according to the captivity of their pride and egos. In our temple endowment play, we had the character Lucifer explain that, "You can buy anything in this world for money."[465] The characters in the play that represent True Messengers (Peter, James, and John) respond to the man Adam:

PETER (to Adam): Do you sell your tokens or signs for money? You have them, I presume.

ADAM: I have them, but I do not sell them for money. I hold them sacred. I am looking for the further light and knowledge Father promised to send me.[466]

[464] *Wikipedia*, "List of wealthiest organizations."
[465] *SNS*, 107.
[466] *SNS*, 107.

The signs and tokens referred to in this scene are those that we plagiarized and copied largely from the Masonic Temple rituals. At the time of this writing, the church that has evolved from Brigham Young has removed many of the "tokens or signs" to which our True Messenger characters are referring (including ALL of the penalties).[467] This important part of our play was "sold out"[468] so that the LDS/Mormon Church could become the wealthiest religion on Earth.[469]

The early European-American Christians rejected our message—the "further light and knowledge Father promised to send."[470] The modern-day American

---

[467] "Penalty (Mormonism)," *Wikipedia, The Free Encyclopedia*, last modified October 15, 2019, https://en.wikipedia.org/wiki/Penalty_(Mormonism). *See also* "Question: Why were 'penalties' removed from the endowment?" *FairMormon*, accessed April 5, 2020, https://www.fairmormon.org/answers/Mormonism_and_temples/Endowment/The_ordinance_versus_the_ritual_used_to_present_the_ordinance#Question:_Why_were_.22penalties.22_removed_from_the_Endowment.3F.
"Temple Penalties and Blood Oaths," *LDS-Mormon.com*, accessed April 5, 2020, http://www.lds-mormon.com/veilworker/penalty.shtml.

[468] *See SNS*, 106–10. The *Merriam-Webster Dictionary* defines "sell out" as "to betray a person or duty," accessed April 4, 2020, https://www.merriam-webster.com/dictionary/sells.

[469] *Wikipedia*, "List of wealthiest organizations."

[470] *SNS, 107.*

Christians are faced with destruction because of the "captivity"[471] of their pride and ego.

Their cognitive paradigms (thinking patterns) fuel the emotional responses that cause depression and hopelessness. They have proven that they follow the "god of this world"[472] the only god that hears and answers their prayers. They are misled and deceived by their leaders who "know not, and know not that they know not."[473] Like the rest of the world, they are asleep.[474]

The world has been lulled away into a deep sleep of ignorance. In spite of the vast amount of knowledge that has been collected over the last 10,000 years, none of the advancements or progressive achievements that have been made have created a better world for the bulk of humanity. For the few, yes. But for the majority, no.

But even for the few, life has become an experience like a dream—in which a hungry man dreams and during the dream he eats until he is full, but when he awakens, he

---

[471] *BOM*, Alma 12:6.
[472] *See BOM*, Mosiah 3:19; *see also SNS*, 87–8, 94–5, 111.
[473] *THOR* (large print), vi.
[474] *THOR* (large print), vi–vii.

finds his soul still feels empty. Or, when a thirsty man dreams that he is drinking water to desperately quench his thirst, but then when he awakens, he is faint. His soul remains thirsty as well as hungry.[475]

Many of the wealthiest and most popular among the few often succumb (submit) to alcohol and drugs as a means to quench the emptiness of their souls.[476] (Today, even the poor majority succumb.)[477] The money, the popularity, and the worldly "treasures" upon which the few feed and drink throughout their lives, fail to satisfy their longing to feel fulfilled and happy. Although they appear to have "everything" (for which the majority also wishes and strives), although they are filled from "eating and drinking," some still choose suicide as a means to assuage the emptiness of their soul.[478]

---

[475] *See* Isaiah 29:8.

[476] Cari Nierenberg, "Rich Kids and Drugs: Addiction May Hit Wealthy Students Hardest," June 1, 2017, https://www.livescience.com/59329-drug-alcohol-addiction-wealthy-students.html.

"List of suicides," *Wikipedia, The Free Encyclopedia*, last modified April 4, 2020, https://en.wikipedia.org/wiki/List_of_suicides.

[477] Editorial Staff, "Addiction among Socioeconomic Groups," *American Addiction Centers*, June 20, 2019, https://sunrisehouse.com/addiction-demographics/socioeconomic-groups.

[478] Nat Berman, "20 Famous Actors Who Committed Suicide," *TVOvermind*, August 10, 2018, https://www.tvovermind.com/actors-who-committed-suicide.

We introduced this human condition in one of the religious writings (scriptures) that we wrote to combat religious influence and deception in the ancient world.[479] It was in this passage that we implied an introduction to our work, in hopes of influencing change in the religious mindsets of the people at that time. We wrote,

It shall even be as when an hungry man dreameth, and, behold, he eateth; but he awaketh, and his soul is empty: or as when a thirsty man dreameth, and, behold, he drinketh; but he awaketh, and, behold, he is faint, and his soul hath appetite: so shall the multitude of all the nations be, that fight against mount Zion.

Stay yourselves, and wonder; cry ye out, and cry: they are drunken, but not with wine; they stagger, but not with strong drink.

---

[479] *THOR* (large print), 115–23.

For the Lord hath poured out upon you the spirit of deep sleep, and hath closed your eyes: the prophets and your rulers, the seers hath he covered.

And the vision of all is become unto you as the words of a book that is sealed, which men deliver to one that is learned, saying, Read this, I pray thee: and he saith, I cannot; for it is sealed:

And the book is delivered to him that is not learned, saying, Read this, I pray thee: and he saith, I am not learned.

Wherefore the Lord said, Forasmuch as this people draw near me with their mouth, and with their lips do honour me, but have removed their heart far from me, and their fear toward me is taught by the precept of men:

Therefore, behold, I will proceed to do a marvellous work among this people, even a marvellous work and a wonder: for the wisdom of their wise men shall perish, and the understanding of their prudent men shall be hid.[480]

When it came time to introduce our new American scripture to the European Christians of the early 19th century (the 1800s), all of whom believed in the King James Bible, we based the name of our work, a Marvelous Work and a Wonder®, on the above passage of biblical scripture. We also included this passage in our new American scripture, the *Book of Mormon*.

Our group (the Real Illuminati™) influenced the author who wrote the original book of Isaiah.[481] Our purpose was to counter the religious movements that

---

[480] Isaiah 29:8–14.
[481] *THOR* (large print), 115–23.

were developing throughout the Eastern Hemisphere during the rise of the Great Roman Empire. In fact, the original book of Isaiah was first written in Greek by Socrates. Socrates[482] had no other purpose in his life other than to counter the developing religions of his day.

About 200 years before Socrates' time, the leaders of a small, developing culture (recognized today as the ancient Hebrews)[483] traveled to Greece in search of writers who could help them pen (compose on paper) their history. Ancient Hebrew history was entirely oral until the time that these Hebrew leaders asked Greek writers to use their skills of storytelling to write their culture's stories.

The divisions that were being experienced in this ancient Hebrew culture motivated Hebrew leaders to organize their oral stories into written form, in hopes of creating more unity in their culture. (Consider the stories about the kingdom of Judah fighting with the kingdom of

---

[482] *THOR* (large print), 107–12.

[483] Harold Hancock, "Is There a Difference Between Hebrews, Jews and Israelites?" *Timberland Drive church of Christ*, accessed April 6, 2020, https://www.timberlandchurch.org/articles/is-there-a-difference-between-hebrews-jews-and-israelites.

Israel, which led to their eventual destruction.)[484] The result was the Greek *Pentateuch* (the *Torah*, the Five Books of Moses).[485]

In spite of their oral stories, none of which can be authenticated as actually occurring, one thing happened that Hebrew storytellers (historians) cannot deny: the complete annihilation of their culture by the Babylonians around 600 BCE.[486]

This was a very humbling time period for the Hebrews. At this time, the Hebrew leaders commissioned Greek writers to write down their oral stories. The Hebrew people needed hope after such a devastating event, when many of them had become slaves to other nations on Earth. The Hebrew traditions and legends about Moses, Abraham, Isaac, and Jacob, provided this hope.

Few of the oral stories that were passed down among the ancient Hebrew culture can be proven today. In Real

---

[484] Owen Jarus, "Biblical Battles: 12 Ancient Wars Lifted from the Bible," *Live Science*, July 24, 2017, https://www.livescience.com/59911-ancient-biblical-battles.html.

[485] "Torah," *Wikipedia, The Free Encyclopedia*, last modified March 19, 2020, https://en.wikipedia.org/wiki/Torah#Greek.

[486] History.com Editors, "Babylonia," *History.com*, last modified August 20, 2019, https://www.history.com/topics/ancient-middle-east/babylonia.

Truth, they are nothing more than legends, myths, or fantastical tales that present the Hebrews as a special culture, more so (according to their stories) than any other.

Again, it is pride and ego (*Lucifer*)[487] that is responsible for a group of people putting themselves above all others on Earth.

The Hebrew leaders now had the first part of their written scripture (Pentateuch/Torah), written in Greek. (The ancient Hebrew language had not yet developed enough for written storytelling.)[488]

In time, as the Hebrew language developed and the Hebrews gained new skills in writing, they wrote more stories about themselves. These focused mainly on putting their culture above all other cultures.

Socrates could see the effect that religious writings had on the Hebrews as he became aware of how prideful

---

[487] *SNS*, 87.

[488] "Hebrew language," *Encyclopædia Britannica*, last modified November 16, 2018, https://www.britannica.com/print/article/259061.

    See also "Biblical Hebrew," *Wikipedia, The Free Encyclopedia*, last modified April 6, 2020, https://en.wikipedia.org/wiki/Biblical_Hebrew; *and*

    "Hebrew language," *Wikipedia, The Free Encyclopedia*, last modified March 31, 2020, https://en.wikipedia.org/wiki/Hebrew_language.

and exclusive their culture had become. Working with us and using our help and influence, Socrates wrote the original book of Isaiah with a pen name. The name that we chose for him at the time was Belzarach.[489]

After Socrates was killed, we were able to introduce the writings of Isaiah to the Hebrew religion in a way that made them believe that Isaiah was a prophet of their God. To prevent our words from being changed by unscrupulous religious leaders, the bulk of the book of Isaiah was written in allegory and poetry.[490] We did the same at a later time with the book of Revelation (500 CE),[491] and with our temple endowment play (1842).[492]

As we explained in our first book, *The True History of Religion*, we counseled Socrates to leave none of his own personal writings. Because of the power that Christianity had in the world at the time of the Great Roman Empire, the actual history of how the Old Testament was written

---

[489] *THOR* (large print), 116.
[490] *THOR*, 112–23.
[491] *THOR* (large print), 144. *See also 666 America*, 110–11.
[492] *SNS*, Preface.

was kept hidden from the masses, most of whom couldn't read or write anyway.

When any religious scripture is written, the most important thing is writing it in such a way that when it is read by a religious person (or is read *to* a religious believer), the reader (or listener) *feels* the spirit of God[493] in its words.

We have learned through experience how to write in order to inspire spiritual emotions that one believes are the promptings of the Holy Spirit. We write according to the beliefs of our intended audience ... "according to the heed and diligence which they give"[494] to that which they believe is the word of God.

Our intent in introducing the writings of Isaiah was to inspire people to care more about the poor and needy among them, than the religion in which they believed. This has always been our number one intent. There is no way

---

[493] *See BOM*, Moroni 7:16.
[494] *See BOM* Alma 12:9.

that peace and goodwill upon Earth can be established until there is "no poor among them."[495]

After the Hebrew culture was destroyed by the Babylonians,[496] they eventually ended up in Palestine, where they began to develop rapidly.[497] This happened only *after* the Great Roman Republic (Empire) had control over that part of the world and helped the Jews to establish their own culture.

The Hebrew culture was very unique compared to many of the other cultures that had developed in the world at that time. It flourished because "they were exceedingly industrious, and they did buy and sell and traffic one with another, that they might get gain."[498]

This hardworking nature of the people came from the Hebrew experience of being slaves to other nations. But as they gained and became industrious, the Hebrews believed

---

[495] *PGP*, Moses 7:18; *see also BOM*, 4 Nephi 1:3.

[496] "Babylonian captivity," *Encyclopedia Britannica*, last modified April 9, 2019, https://www.britannica.com/event/Babylonian-Captivity.

[497] "Jewish History," *Wikipedia, The Free Encyclopedia*, last modified April 5, 2020, https://en.wikipedia.org/wiki/Jewish_history.

[498] *Compare BOM*, Ether 10:22; *see also BOM*, Alma 23:18.

that their prosperity was a result of the blessings they received from their God:

> And never could be a people more blessed than were they, and more prospered by the hand of the Lord. And they were in a land that was choice above all lands, for the Lord had spoken it.[499]

The Mormons of Joseph Smith's time were not much different from the Hebrew's of ancient times. Once we realized that the intended audience of our new scripture had rejected the "mark"[500] of the everlasting Gospel as "delivered by the Savior to the ancient inhabitants,"[501] we added a new subplot to our storyline. This subplot, presented in what we called the *Plates of Nephi*, introduced a great nation of white-skinned people that once controlled all of North America: the Great Jaredite Nation.

---

[499] *BOM*, Ether 10:28.
[500] *BOM*, Jacob 4:14.
[501] *PGP*, JSH 1:34.

The Jaredite story was meant to allegorically represent the Great United States of America, a nation controlled by fair-skinned people.

The story began in the Eastern Hemisphere and dovetailed the Bible story about the Tower of Babel.[502] From there, we incorporated many other Bible stories, changing the names of the characters to fit our Jaredite narrative. The story of Moses receiving the word of God on a mountain[503] was copied to present our own character, *the brother of Jared*, receiving God's will for his own people.[504]

According to the Bible's narrative, the Great Flood killed all that was living. So there could not have been any living animals upon the Western Hemisphere afterwards. We used the story of Noah and the Ark[505] as a model for us to explain how the Jaredites transferred animals and seeds from the Eastern Hemisphere to the Western.[506]

---

[502] *BOM*, Introduction.
[503] Exodus 34:28.
[504] *BOM*, Ether, 3:1 through 4:1.
[505] Exodus, chapter 7.
[506] *BOM*, Ether, chapter 2.

But something very important that we did *not* include in our Jaredite narrative was any type of organized or structured religion ... <u>of any kind</u>.

The Jaredites had no churches, no temples,[507] no religious rituals, and no priesthood authority or structure, even though the *brother of Jared* had received his instructions from God on the mountain.

To reiterate the importance of Jesus, the Christ, in our narrative, we presented the God with whom the brother of Jared communicated as Jesus.

We will give more details about the Jaredite story in one of the chapters of our book, *A New American Scripture—How and Why the Real Illuminati™ Created the Book of Mormon.*

As we have explained, the early American Christians rejected our message that no religion should be part of the correct type of society, of the right form of government. But because Christianity was so powerful and controlling

---

[507] "Nowhere in all the words of Christ, either in the *Book of Mormon* or the Bible, can there be found any instructions or commandments regarding the construction of temples or the performing of special ordinances therein." *SNS*, 3.

over the hearts and minds of the people, we were forced to use this religion as the basis of our story's plot.

This plot presented the "FULNESS OF THE EVERLASTING GOSPEL,"[508] or rather, that upon which a society should base its laws, morals, and ethics, as the proper way to "serve God."[509]

The words that our new American scripture's Jesus delivered to the ancient inhabitants of the Western Hemisphere, had nothing to do with organized religion. **This "fulness" was all about treating others correctly.** With this in mind, we warned the early Americans (white-skinned European Christians) about their actions as they (the Gentiles) occupied this new, Western Hemisphere, the "land of promise":[510]

> And now, we can behold the decrees of God concerning this land, that it is a land of promise; and whatsoever nation shall possess it shall serve

---

[508] *PGP*, JSH 1:34.
[509] *BOM*, 3 Nephi 5:3.
[510] *BOM*, Ether 2:9.

God, or they shall be swept off when the fulness of his wrath shall come upon them. And the fulness of his wrath cometh upon them when they are ripened in iniquity.

For behold, this is a land which is choice above all other lands; wherefore he that doth possess it shall serve God or shall be swept off; for it is the everlasting decree of God. And it is not until the fulness of iniquity among the children of the land, that they are swept off.

And this cometh unto you [*i.e., the story of the Jaredites*], O ye Gentiles, that ye may know the decrees of God—that ye may repent, and not continue in your iniquities until the fulness come, that ye may not bring down the fulness of the wrath of God upon you as the inhabitants of the land have hitherto done.

Behold, this is a choice land, and whatsoever nation shall possess it shall be free from bondage, and from captivity, and from all other nations under heaven, if they will but serve the God of the land, who is Jesus Christ, who hath been manifested by the things which we have written.[511]

We tried to make it very clear in our 1842 play[512] that <u>all</u> religion, of every kind, along with <u>all</u> religious writings—scripture "mingled with the philosophies of men"—are from the "god of this world,"[513] Lucifer—from our human pride and ego. But those who saw it didn't understand. They couldn't comprehend that there is no other source of religious belief other than *Lucifer* ... one's pride and ego. There is no other source of revelation and inspiration. Nor is there any other influence or energy outside of an individual's own brain's cognitive functions.

---

[511] *BOM*, Ether 2:9–12.
[512] *Sacred, not Secret*, https://www.realilluminati.org/sacred-not-secret.
[513] *See SNS*, 87; *see also BOM*, Mosiah 3:19.

We know this. We can prove this, and have proved it many times in our associations with others. Some of the greatest proof of this, however, is how we wrote our new scripture for the early Americans, and when necessary, changed it to conform to the *feelings* of the reader.[514]

Anyone who can write *believable* religious scripture has to know what they're doing. Or at the very least, know what a person who reads scripture (or has scripture read to them) wants to hear that will make the person feel like the information is the word of God—a personal message from God for the individual.

Spiritual feelings, thought to be from God, are also sometimes associated with evil, eerie feelings, which are associated with the devil. An example of these types of feelings being simple functions of the normal brain instead of from an outside source, is when one of our contemporary messengers commented on an alleged exorcism. "Give him some weed [marijuana] and watch how fast the devil

---

[514] *See BOM*, 1 Nephi 19:1–5.

leaves."[515] It is an undisputed Real Truth that a person who appears to be possessed by the devil can be given a sedative and the evil spirit will "miraculously" depart.

Nevertheless, one who has experienced a strong *spiritual* event, one who has seen a spirit, an angel, or a demon, will hardly be convinced that the event was all made up in their head. This reluctance to acknowledge the actual source of all spiritual feelings (good or evil) will usually always be the case, unless the person speaks to someone "who knows, and knows that they know."[516] A *true* wise one uses sound logic and common sense to explain these emotional feelings as nothing more than the normal functioning power of the human brain.

This is, in every case, the Real Truth about *spiritual feelings*.

There are billions of people throughout the world who can testify of a spiritual experience that convinced them that God is real; or rather, that they felt an overwhelming

---

[515] "The Man From Joe's Bar and Grill, The Autobiography of Christopher Marc Nemelka," *Real Illuminati*™, accessed April 2, 2020, https://www.realilluminati.org/the-man-from-joe-s-bar-and-grill.
[516] *THOR* (large print), vi–vii.

real feeling that could not have come from inside their own head. Although the human brain cannot *feel* without itself functioning and creating a feeling, billions are still convinced that something outside of their own brain can cause their brain to feel.

What is not logically considered is the ability of the brain to produce *feelings* that *cause* the *spiritual feeling*. But what causes the brain to produce these feelings that *feel like* they're coming from another source?

It's about *how* the story is told. It's about what the brain sees, hears, smells, tastes, and touches.

Over the many millennia that humans have existed, religious storytellers (scripture writers) and leaders have learned how to make the unsuspecting brain feel these feelings.

So did we.

When a person walks into a great and spacious religious church, cathedral, or massive temple, the person *feels* small. With their *eyes*, they see how small they really are compared to the vastness of the building, which they have been told is the "house of God." Their ears can hear the echoes of vastness. Even their own voice succumbs to the enormous expanse, and they find themselves whispering in hypnotic reverence for the place. If in their childhood, the practice of lighting a candle to represent God's light was a part of their upbringing, then the *sight and smell* of lighting a candle in the church reminds them that they have entered into "God's house."

These feelings are real. We will never dispute this. We cannot. Nevertheless, these feelings are the result of a person's pride and ego, the basic structural standard of the mortal brain, which we call *Lucifer* ... nothing more, nothing less.

How proud is the one who can actually walk into "God's house" and be accepted there? How proud is the one who feels like the most powerful entity in the universe (God) is aware of their presence and cares for them? How proud is the one who feels *special* because God pays attention and hears and answers their personal prayers and pleas?

That's the key to properly understanding where these spiritual feelings come from… human pride and ego.

That which makes each of us feel proud is the same thing that makes each of us human. To properly understand what creates pride and ego, we need to consider little children.

Do little children know who God is? Do they know who the devil is? Do they need a Savior?

Our common sense should help us understand that children are not born into this world with any preconditioned or preprogrammed concept about religion, spirituality, or anything else *outside* of their own immediate experience and needs.

If humankind needs a Savior who died for their sins, what sin has a little child committed that would cause the child to need a Savior?

Because this was a very contentious argument among the Catholic and Protestant Christian faiths at the time we wrote our new scripture, we were forced to address this argument.[517] While addressing it, we also explained that a non-religious human does not need a Savior either.[518]

It was not our desire at the time we were finishing our storyline to deal with the issue of infant baptism or baptism for the dead, or many other issues that we were forced to address because those whom Joseph Smith allowed to review our story remained confused. It was our intent to end our story with the destruction of the powerful white-skinned Jaredite nation,[519] as a warning to the early American Christians as they began to develop their own nation in "the promised land."[520]

We intended to end our revised story with the reader wondering about other ancient records that might come forth in the future. We did this so that we could produce other future writings, if needed. This was also accomplished in our main storyline, in the introduction of

---

[517] *BOM*, Moroni 8:5–24.
[518] *BOM*, Moroni 8:22.
[519] *See BOM*, Ether chapters 1, 14–15.
[520] *BOM*, 1 Nephi 13:12–13.

the "sealed" part,[521] the "greater portion of the word,"[522] which we eventually published as *The Sealed Portion—The Final Testament of Jesus Christ* (2004).[523]

We wanted to leave the reader wondering about more writings ("and the hundredth part I have not written,")[524] and also wondering about the existence of those who were "translated,"[525] or rather, whose brains have been *transfigured* [526] as we presented in our storyline through the characters the "Three Nephites" and "John, the Beloved."[527]

To leave the impression that there might be others, Ether's final words implied that he might "be translated."[528]

Here's how we first expected to end our *Book of Mormon* story:

---

[521] *BOM*, 2 Nephi, chapter 27.

[522] *BOM*, Alma 12:10.

[523] *The Sealed Portion*, https://www.realilluminati.org/the-sealed-portion.

[524] *BOM*, Ether 15:33.

[525] *BOM*, Ether 15:34.

[526] *THOR* (large print), 31.

[527] *See BOM*, 3 Nephi, chapter 28.

[528] *BOM*, Ether 15:34.

Ether is our character who represents a True Messenger sent to the Jaredite people to call them to repentance. He was rejected and hid in a

> cavity of a rock by day, and by night he went forth viewing the things which should come upon the [Jaredites]. And as he dwelt in the cavity of a rock he made the remainder of this record, viewing the destructions which came upon the people.[529]

The Jaredite plot ends with only two of the leaders left, fighting each other with swords. One kills the other, and then only two people are left of the once-great white-skinned Jaredite nation: Ether (our True Messenger) and Coriantumr, the last great Jaredite king.[530]

The "people of Limhi" mentioned below are the ones who would eventually find Ether's record hundreds of years later.

---

[529] *See BOM*, Ether 13:12–14.
[530] *See BOM*, Ether 15:29–33.

And the Lord spake unto Ether, and said unto him: Go forth. And he went forth, and beheld that the words of the Lord had all been fulfilled; and he finished his record; (and the hundredth part I have not written) and he hid them in a manner that the people of Limhi did find them. Now the last words which are written by Ether are these: Whether the Lord will that I be translated, or that I suffer the will of the Lord in the flesh, it mattereth not, if it so be that I am saved in the kingdom of God. Amen.[531]

According to our story, the ancient native American ancestors, traveling from South America to "the land northward," encountered the aftermath of the destroyed Jaredite Nation. They discovered Jaredite

bones of men, and of beasts, and [the land] was also covered with ruins of building of every kind,

---

[531] *See BOM*, Ether 15:33–4.

having discovered a land which had been peopled with a people who were as numerous as the hosts of Israel. And for a testimony ... they have brought twenty-four plates which are filled with engravings, and they are of pure gold.[532]

Again, we introduced the story of the *destruction* of the Jaredites, ONLY AFTER our original plot was rejected by those who reviewed the first 116 pages of the original handwritten manuscript.

We intended to give the American people an idea of what *might* become of their new nation in the example of the Jaredites. It was our hope that the Americans would understand the corrupt nature of organized religion. Had our original plot not been rejected, we would have written the Jaredite story in a different way. We would have had the people develop a righteous nation. And in the Jaredite record, we would have provided a blueprint for this righteous nation. It would have been an example

---

[532] *BOM*, Mosiah 8:8–9.

of a great nation of people who were following the commands of the god that first spoke with the first Jaredite leader, the brother of Jared: the words and direction of *our* Jesus Christ.

Because we didn't know exactly how our story was going to be received, in our *original storyline* we clued the reader in on the manner in which our story was being written:

> For behold, I, Mormon, do not know beforehand what I am about to write in the abridgment that I am engraving upon these plates of ore [as the *Book of Mormon*]. Nevertheless, this I do know: that the Spirit of God is within me and I write those things which God wants to preserve for those who will find these plates and bring forth the words which I have written.[533]

Mormon was the main engraver (storyteller) on the plates that would become our *Book of Mormon*. After

---

[533] *TSP*, Lehi 9:24.

introducing how he was (we were) writing the story, according to what "the Spirit of God"[534] told him to write, we left the door open for whatever it was that we wanted to present to our early American readers ... what we *had* to present in order to get them to believe in our *new American scripture.*

After our original storyline was rejected, it was our desire to leave the American reader with a dire warning of destruction, according to the example of the Great Jaredite Nation, if they (the Gentiles) did not run their nation correctly.

But after Joseph Smith allowed his peers to review what we intended for the final chapter in our book, they were still confused. We were forced to once again add an addendum.

Wherefore, I write a few more things, contrary to that which I had supposed; for I had supposed not to have written any more; but I write a few more things, that perhaps they may be of worth unto

---

[534] *TSP*, Lehi 9:24.

my brethren, the Lamanites, in some future day, according to the will of the Lord.[535]

Joseph's peers were confused about the lack of instructions given by Jesus in our story. As mentioned above, they were still confused about some controversial issues that were not covered, i.e., infant baptism and baptism for the dead.

The people "looked beyond the mark"[536] of the words of our Jesus and wanted an organized religion. We gave them what they wanted.[537] We amended our original storyline to include how the Holy Ghost is given to a person,[538] how a church's priesthood should be conferred and operate,[539] and how baptisms and church meetings should be conducted.[540]

---

[535] *BOM*, Moroni 1:4.

[536] *BOM*, Jacob 4:14.

[537] *JS Bio*, 14. *See also THOR* (large print), 227. *JS Bio*, 430: "God had given the people what they wanted so that they would stumble; for in stumbling they would come to understand and appreciate the words of Christ by experiencing what occurs when they are ignored."

[538] *BOM*, Moroni, chapter 2.

[539] *BOM*, Moroni, chapter 3.

[540] *BOM*, Moroni, chapters 4–6.

We provided an explanation of the hypocrisy that was possible for the members of a church.[541] We then introduced important clues about the true nature of Christ, hoping that our explanation would satisfy the people's longing for a Savior.

We gave a detailed explanation about the "Spirit of Christ,"[542] or the "light of Christ."[543] As clearly as we could, we explained that every person on Earth has this same "spirit" and "light"—that it is the mortal human conscience that makes us *feel* what is right and what it wrong.[544]

We tried to end our story on the idea of a person becoming like Christ "according to the words of Christ";[545] and that the "pure love of Christ"[546] was the most important thing. We wrote what we had hoped would be our final message given in our *Book of Mormon*.

---

[541] *BOM*, Moroni, chapter 7.
[542] *BOM*, Moroni 7:16–17.
[543] *BOM*, Moroni 7:18–19.
[544] *BOM*, Moroni 7:12–19.
[545] *BOM*, Moroni 7:38.
[546] *BOM*, Moroni 7:47.

This final message countered the religious organization and priesthood that we allowed Joseph Smith to introduce, because the people rejected "the fulness of the everlasting Gospel ... as delivered by the Savior."[547]

In the *Book of Mormon,* chapter seven of Moroni made the "love of Christ" the most important attribute that a person needed to have so that "at the last day, it shall be well with him."[548]

The "Spirit"[549] or the "light" of Christ[550] (charity)[551] has nothing do with religion. It has <u>all</u> to do with those qualities that everyone knows are good and are attributes of a kind person:

> And charity suffereth long, and is kind, and envieth not, and is not puffed up, seeketh not her own, is not easily provoked, thinketh no evil, and rejoiceth not in iniquity but rejoiceth in the truth,

---

[547] *PGP,* JSH 1:34.
[548] *BOM,* Moroni 7:47.
[549] *BOM,* Moroni 7:16–17.
[550] *BOM,* Moroni 7:18–19.
[551] *BOM,* Moroni 7:44–6.

beareth all things, believeth all things, hopeth all things, endureth all things. [*We were describing the attributes of a little child.*]

Wherefore, my beloved brethren, if ye have not charity, ye are nothing, for charity never faileth. Wherefore, cleave unto charity, which is the greatest of all, for all things must fail [*including all religions and religious beliefs*]—But charity is the pure love of Christ, and it endureth forever; and whoso is found possessed of it at the last day, it shall be well with him. Wherefore, my beloved brethren, pray unto the Father with all the energy of heart, that ye may be filled with this love, which he hath bestowed upon all who are true followers of his Son, Jesus Christ; that ye may become the sons of God; that when he shall appear we shall be like him, for we shall see him as he is; that we may have this hope; that we may be purifed even as he is pure. Amen.[552]

Astonishingly, the early Americans to whom Joseph showed our *completed* record (as we supposed) had other questions and concerns.

We were forced to continue the storyline:

And now, my son, I speak unto you concerning that which grieveth me exceedingly; for it grieveth me that there should disputations rise among you. For, if I have learned the truth, there have been disputations among you concerning the baptism of your little children.[553]

We thought that understanding why infants didn't need baptism would be easy ... because an infant doesn't have the capability to sin. To make sure it was properly understood, we added a significant addendum to this conclusion. We

---

[552] *BOM*, Moroni 7:45–8.
[553] *BOM*, Moroni 8:4–5.

explained that "all they that are without the law"[554] are like little children and do not need baptism or a Savior.

In other words, all non-religious people who do not have the "law of God"[555] taught to them—as religious people suppose is taught to them by their religious leaders—do *not* need a Savior.

How can a person, who does not know that it is a sin to do something, be punished for doing something that nobody told the person was wrong?

Does a person who already has the "Spirit of Christ" ("given to every man")[556] need to be baptized? Does a person need to be "saved," if they live their life without religion, and yet is a person, who

suffers long, and is kind, and doesn't envy, is not puffed up, doesn't seek her own, is not easily provoked, thinks no evil, and does not rejoice in iniquity but rejoices in truth, who bears all

---

[554] *BOM*, Moroni 8:22.
[555] *BOM*, Moroni 8:22.
[556] *See BOM*, Moroni 7:16.

things, believes all things, hopes all things, and endures all things?[557]

No! They do not! We tried to make this important point perfectly clear to the early American Christians (those who read our story, and were convinced that it was *divine* and of God). Instead of accepting this concept as a true concept, they rejected every idea and perspective that we tried to introduce.

In modern times, the religion that holds our book as the cornerstone of its church mocks our teachings.

The LDS/Mormon Church does not accept that there are good people in the world who are kind, naturally reflecting the "light of Christ,"[558] without knowing Christ, being baptized, or joining a religion. Instead, this church sends out thousands of missionaries[559] to tell the people the "laws of God," as they suppose. They condemn the

---

[557] *Compare BOM*, Moroni 7:45–8.
[558] *BOM*, Moroni 7:18–19.
[559] "Facts and Statistics," *The Church of Jesus Christ of Latter-day Saints*, accessed April 6, 2020, https://newsroom.churchofjesuschrist.org/facts-and-statistics.

people to whom they proselyte, when *their* laws of God are rejected by "those who are without law."[560]

Furthermore, this church deceives its followers, perverting the intent of our words, that anyone who has died "without law"[561] needs to receive the church ordinances of baptism in order to be saved.[562]

Modern Mormons metaphorically spit in our face, reject our doctrine, and are under just as much condemnation as those who baptize infants.

> Wo be unto them that shall pervert the ways of the Lord after this manner, for they shall perish except they repent.[563]
>
> ...
>
> For behold that all little children are alive in Christ, and also all they that are without the law. For the power of redemption cometh on all them that have

[560] *See BOM*, Moroni 8:22.
[561] *BOM*, Moroni 8:22.
[562] "Baptism for the Dead," *The Church of Jesus Christ of Latter-day Saints*, accessed April 4, 2020, https://newsroom.churchofjesuschrist.org/article/baptism-for-the-dead.
[563] *BOM*, Moroni 8:16.

no law; wherefore, he that is not condemned, or he that is under no condemnation, cannot repent; and unto such baptism availeth nothing—But it is mockery before God, denying the mercies of Christ, and the power of his Holy Spirit, and putting trust in dead works [*genealogy and work for the dead who died without law are "dead works"*]. Behold, my son, this thing ought not to be; for repentance is unto them that are under condemnation and under the curse of a broken law.[564]

Modern Latter-day Saints/Mormons openly mock God, according to our teachings, in their "dead works," because of their genealogy and temple work (baptism) for the dead ... "for those who died without law."[565]

We included a clear explanation that genealogies and any concern for one's ancestors, although "pleasing unto

---

[564] *BOM*, Moroni 8:22–4.
[565] *BOM*, Moroni 8:22.

the world," are not "pleasing unto God and unto those who are not of the world."[566]

They mock God by their belief in plural marriage. Even when we made it perfectly clear in our story that, "there shall not any man among you have save it be one wife; and concubines he shall have none."[567]

Under Brigham Young's corrupt administration, plural marriage was made the highest priesthood ordinance to which a male could attain a Celestial Glory.[568]

We wrote in our *Book of Mormon:*

And now I make an end of speaking unto you concerning this pride [*Lucifer*]. And were it not that I must speak unto you concerning a grosser crime, my heart would rejoice exceedingly because of you.[569]

---

[566] *See BOM*, 1 Nephi, chapter 6.
[567] *BOM*, Jacob 2:27.
[568] "The only men who become Gods, even the Sons of God, are those who enter into polygamy," Brigham Young, *Journal of Discourses* (Liverpool: B. Young, June 1867), 11:269.
　　To understand the truth about polygamy and Mormonism, *see JS Bio*, Appendix 2, "Mormon Polygamy—The Truth Revealed!" 638–75.
[569] *BOM*, Jacob 2:22.

This "grosser crime" is plural marriage.

We couldn't have written any clearer, so we assumed, that plural marriage was a "gross crime" and an "abomination before God."[570]

How could we have made it any clearer that plural marriage:

[breaks] the hearts of your tender wives, and [loses] the confidence of your children, because of your bad examples before them; and the sobbings of their hearts ascend up to God against you[?][571]

The Mormons still believe (mostly in secret because it is not popular in the "eyes of the world")[572] that plural marriage[573] will be reinstituted upon Earth during the millennial reign of *their* Christ and God.[574]

---

[570] *See BOM*, Jacob 2:22–35.

[571] *BOM*, Jacob 2:35.

[572] *BOM*, 1 Nephi 22:23.

[573] "Plural Marriage and Families in Early Utah," *The Church of Jesus Christ of Latter-day Saints*, accessed April 2, 2020, https://www.churchofjesuschrist.org/topics/plural-marriage-and-families-in-early-utah.

[574] *See for example*: Gramps, "Polygamy in the millennium," *Ask Gramps*, April 23, 2011, https://askgramps.org/polygamy-in-the-millenium/. *See also* McConkie, *Mormon Doctrine*, 410.

As one can see, *their* Christ and God will tell them anything that they need to hear in order to sustain their pride in belonging to the "only true and living church of God upon Earth:"[575] Lucifer's (i.e., their pride and ego's) church, the "church of the devil," the "great and abominable church"[576] supported by Capitalism.

This church, that eventually became one of the wealthiest religions in the world,[577] openly mocks our story. But no one can deny the spiritual *feeling* he or she receives when they read our book (the *Book of Mormon)*. Even so, these spiritual feelings deceive them into trusting their leaders.

Their religion and belief in continuing revelation from God through priesthood lines of authority (only given to men) has completely replaced our new scripture.[578]

---

[575] Oaks, "The Only True and Living Church."

[576] *BOM*, 1 Nephi, chapters 13–14.

[577] *Wikipedia*, "List of wealthiest organizations."

[578] *See* "Divine Revelation in Modern Times," *The Church of Jesus Christ of Latter-day Saints*, December 12, 2011, https://newsroom.churchofjesuschrist.org/article/divine-revelation-modern-times;

Jeffrey R. Holland, "God's Words Never Cease: The Bible, the Book of Mormon, and Continuing Revelation," *The Church of Jesus Christ of Latter-day Saints*, July 14, 2009, https://www.youtube.com/watch?v=K_xl_AR0IRs;

Other concerns that we had to deal with before we finally ended our story had to do with religious gifts, healings, speaking in tongues, and other spiritual miracles.[579]

We made it very clear that, unless a person has *charity* (the Spirit and light of Christ,[580] the pure love of Christ),[581] a person can have no such gift.[582] We did this with purpose in order to have religiously induced people seek more to become a good person, full of the traits we listed as those of one who has the "pure love of Christ,"[583] rather than envying spiritual gifts or receiving miracles.

When we had Joseph introduce the first 116 pages of our book of Lehi, we intended to debunk the idea that the native American peoples, as well as Africans and other darker-skinned races, had been "cursed by God" with a dark skin, as orthodox Bible-based religions taught.

"The Church of Jesus Christ," *The Church of Jesus Christ of Latter-day Saints*, accessed April 5, 2020, https://www.churchofjesuschrist.org/church/organization/the-church-of-jesus-christ.
[579] *BOM*, Moroni 10:8–19.
[580] *BOM*, Moroni 7:18–19.
[581] *BOM*, Moroni 7:47.
[582] *BOM*, Moroni 10:17–25.
[583] *BOM*, Moroni 7:47.

We originally wrote:

And the Nephites were an industrious people who engaged in all manner of commerce and industry for the benefit of all the people.

And the Lamanites became lazy and adulterous and would not wear clothes to cover their naked bodies, thus allowing the sun to change their skin to a darkness that was passed on to their children. And after each generation, the skin of the Lamanites and their children became darker, evensomuch that there began to be a great distinction between the Nephites and the Lamanites.

For behold, the Nephites wore clothing that protected their bodies from the light of the sun, therefore, they were a white and delightsome people.

But because of their wickedness, the Lamanites developed a tolerance to the light of the sun and in this way darkened their own bodies. And thus were they fulfilling the words of Lehi that he prophesied against them saying: Oh, my pain is great because of the visions I have had concerning Laman and Lemuel. For the Lord hath shown me the curse that shall come upon them, even that they shall become a dark and loathsome people, except they repent and obey the commandments of the Lord.[584]

The Americans rejected this idea because of the Bible and its implication that darker-skinned races were cursed by God with a dark skin, stemming from the curse of Cain.[585] Our proposed concept (that the sun had actually made them dark through natural law) was rejected outright, which caused a few readers to completely reject the rest of our story. They wouldn't continue reading our scripture when

---

[584] *TSP*, Lehi 7:14–17.
[585] *See* Genesis, chapter 4, especially verses 11 and 15.

they learned that there was no actual curse. For this reason, when we rewrote the story, we were forced to include this Bible-based prejudiced view of darker-skinned peoples.[586]

Many American Christians had been converted to the church that was organized because of our book. Nevertheless, by 1842, just twelve years after our book was published as the *Book of Mormon*, it was very evident to us that they had perverted and corrupted our intended message. For this reason, we instructed Joseph Smith to present our 1842 play[587] to them, according to the words that we had written long ago for Isaiah:

(Below is the correct translation from the original Greek, transposed with the King James Bible version.)

Go, and tell this people, Ye hear indeed, but ye do not understand; and ye see indeed, but perceive not that which ye see.

---

[586] For an example, *see BOM*, Alma 3:6.
[587] *JS Bio*, 23–5, 535–7.

Therefore thou shalt give unto them that for which they seek, and those things which they do not understand, for they seek to hear heavy things, and their hearts are full of excess because they desire that which maketh their ears heavy, even that which they do not understand. Preach unto them much and make their ears heavy with your preaching; yea, make the heart of this people fat in that which they desire, but shut their eyes to the truth that would heal them; For they are a fallen people who seek not the Lord to establish his righteousness so that they see with their eyes, and hear with their ears, and understand with their heart, and convert, and be healed.[588]

We gave this same clue in other words after we were forced to rewrite the first part of our story:

---

[588] *Compare* Isaiah 6:9–10.

But behold, the Jews were a stiffnecked people; and they despised the words of plainness, and killed the prophets, and sought for things that they could not understand. Wherefore, because of their blindness, which blindness came by looking beyond the mark, they must needs fall; for God hath taken away his plainness from them, and delivered unto them many things which they cannot understand, because they desired it. And because they desired it God hath done it, that they may stumble.[589]

As we have mentioned, neither the LDS/Mormons nor their leaders understand our play (known as the LDS Temple Endowment Presentation).[590]

The modern people, who believe that our *Book of Mormon* is another "word of God"[591] and who have made our

---

[589] *BOM*, Jacob 4:14.
[590] "About the Temple Endowment," https://www.churchofjesuschrist.org/temples/what-is-temple-endowment.
[591] *PGP*, Articles of Faith 1:8.

play their most sacred temple ordinance,[592] have completely rejected and transfigured our story's intended message.

As we proceed to unfold how and why we wrote the *Book of Mormon* the way that we did, it will become very obvious how we did everything that we could to inspire the acceptance of various ideas and doctrines that could help heal humanity. In almost every case, the LDS/Mormons refused to see and accept what we were presenting as the "fulness of the everlasting Gospel,"[593] and instead corrupted our message.

As you read our words, set aside all prejudice and subjective (biased) perceptions. USE YOUR COMMON SENSE. Use reason and logic as your guide, the "Spirit of Christ,"[594] the "light of Christ,"[595] our conscience—that which makes all of us equally human and helps us to know right from wrong.

---

[592] "Temple Endowment," *The Church of Jesus Christ of Latter-day Saints*, accessed April 6, 2020, https://www.churchofjesuschrist.org/study/history/topics/temple-endowment.
[593] *PGP*, JSH 1:34.
[594] *BOM*, Moroni 7:16–17.
[595] *BOM*, Moroni 7:18–19.

Using common sense, you will discover that we know how to write scripture in such a way that when religious people read it, they *feel* something that *feels* like an outside source is revealing the truth to them ... like God is giving them evidence of truth.

Actually, this feeling is created by the brain as it remembers something that was once forgotten, but has been brought to a person's remembrance.

Consider some of Joseph Smith's last words, meant for the spiritually or religious-minded:

When our Christ visited me as a young boy, he taught me of this eternal equality. He was not the Christ that the world accepted and imagined at the time. I was instructed in his true nature at this time. By this nature, I learned of our mutual equality. I learned that his purpose was to ensure this equality by overseeing the existence of the mortals who belong to this earth, who will one day exist as he does, equal to him in eternal glory.

I learned that mortality was an experience of inequality that provided us with the opportunity to gain an appreciation of our eternal state.

My commission under Christ was to work with others, similarly assigned, to provide mortals with a chance to find the power of their minds that would redeem them to their original state of equality. They did not easily discover the things hidden in their minds because of the inequality that exists in their mortality. I was to dwell among them sharing equal imperfections of a fallen nature but with nothing hidden in my mind. I had a perfect recollection of the eternal nature of all things.

I was taught and aided by others in how to exist among them without disclosing the differences and inequalities of our minds. Everything we did was for their benefit, that their minds might become equal again with ours. If I were allowed to reveal the things that had been hid from them, then they would not understand our mutual equality. I would be above them, not by my own will, but by their desire.

In hope that they would discover the answers on their own, we provided clues for them. But they did not perceive the clues, choosing instead to continue the inequality of their minds, an inequality patterned after their mortal state, unaffected by the immortal yearnings of their souls. But in this, they did not fail. They proved the need for a Christ, who is and shall always be, the great equalizer of humankind, making all equal with him, redeeming all from their fallen state.

The fullness of the everlasting Gospel is the idea of equality in all things. Mortals reject this idealistic concept because of the fallen state in which they exist. But they once accepted it, and will once again after they have experienced a trial of their existence without it.[596]

When we think about a past event in our life, our brain creates *feelings* about the event as we think about it. These feelings do not come from our present situation, although it is in the present that we remember the event. The present feelings surrounding the *past* event almost feel like they are coming from a source outside of our brain, when these *feelings* are actually being created *by* our brain as we remember the event.

So it is with the Real Truth of all things.

When we hear Real Truth, it makes complete sense. It seems logical and reasonable according to our natural ability to reason.

Problems arise through "cognitive dissonance,"[597] when what we believe does not agree with what makes sense. This is when pride enters and does not allow us to

---

[596] *JS Bio*, "Epilogue," 585.

[597] "Cognitive dissonance," *Wikipedia, The Free Encyclopedia*, last modified March 29, 2020, https://en.wikipedia.org/wiki/Cognitive_dissonance.

accept that which makes more sense than what we have been taught to believe.

Humans do not want to be wrong. Humans want to believe that there is a source of all Real Truth, and that they have access to this source; that they are *proudly* privileged to have this source. Thus, *Lucifer* (our pride and ego) tells us and introduces us to his worldly Ministers (those who tell us things that make us proud to be part of an organized religion).

Convinced that they are not equal with others who claim to know what they don't (i.e., ministers: religious leaders, spiritual advisers, etc.), religious followers *believe* what they are told by their accepted religious leaders, even if it doesn't make any sense. They accept these leaders and teachers as their representatives of truth. Once they have accepted that what they are told as true, then anything their religious leaders tell them automatically produces the *feelings* that they relate to spiritual things from God.

Children are taught that they must accept other people as their teachers. This was not how humans were born, however. We are all born with an equal access to the "light of Christ,"[598] that comes from within, which we refer to as the common sense and understanding of Real Truth.

Little children do not listen to anyone or anything outside of their own invention, UNTIL they are inculcated (indoctrinated) by reward and punishment.

It is not natural for a human to listen to anyone but their own self. It *is* natural for someone to hear the Real Truth and recognize it, as a little child would.

But as children are rewarded for listening to others outside of themselves, or punished for not listening to such, their minds are affected and conditioned to listening to something *outside* of their own brain. This is why people *feel* the presence of God, or the inspiration of God, when they listen to their leaders and teachers. Adults have forgotten how to rely on their *own* brain as a source of knowledge, as they did when they were little children.

---

[598] *BOM*, Moroni 7:18–19.

In our 1842 play,[599] we had the character who represents a True Messenger say to Adam—the character intended to represent all mortals,

> Adam, we are true messengers from the Father, and have come to give you the further light and knowledge He promised to send you.

[To which Adam responds,]

How shall I know that you are true messengers?[600]

The true messenger character proceeds to tell Adam that he will "[give] unto [him] the token and sign [he] received in the Garden of Eden."[601]

We explained in our new American scripture that all humans are born with the same and equal "Spirit of Christ,"[602] which is their conscience.

---

[599] *Sacred, not Secret*, https://www.realilluminati.org/sacred-not-secret.
[600] *SNS*, 121.
[601] *SNS*, 121.
[602] *BOM*, Moroni 7:16.

The term, "REAL TRUTH" can replace the "Spirit of Christ," or any other mention of Christ in our writings, and the meaning will be the same as we intended to present it allegorically.

The way to tell if you hear the Real Truth is that it cannot be disputed by using *common sense* and *reason*—uniquely human attributes. You will know that we are presenting the Real Truth because what we present makes more sense than what you might believe. If what you believe does not make as much sense as the Real Truth, your human sense of *reason* should convince you that what you believe is not correct.

As we dealt with the young Joseph Smith, we explained to him that he should *not* tell the people the Real Truth about what he knew; that he should not "[disclose his true] identity."[603]

When we reveal the Real Truth surrounding the events that led to the publication of our new American scripture, *logic* and *reason* will be the proof that the

---

[603] *SNS*, 95; *JS Bio*, "Appendix 3," 676–80.

reader will have that will convince the reader that we are True Messengers.

There are always two sides to every issue. There are those who believe in our new American scripture and those who don't. *Truth* is established by each side, not necessarily according to Real Truth (i.e., events as they *really* happened) but, more often than not, according to the emotional slant and bias taken by each. Each side can find supporting evidence, documentation, and "facts" that support its truth.

When a person is curious about something and makes an honest effort to find out the truth, objective neutrality can be threatened by the strong emotional fight that each side of the *facts* makes to defend its own truth.

We have coined the statement, "Everyone is right. Which makes everyone wrong.®"

So how does one find the truth?

How does one know that we are True Messengers?

As we have explained, humans have special tools that are unique to our species and can help us find Real Truth: logic and reason.

Logic deals with the principles and criteria of what one might consider to be true, based on <u>actual</u> events that support what is considered to be true. *Reason* is the ability to determine if the events were *actual*.

Shortly after Joseph Smith Jr. was murdered on June 27, 1844, Brigham Young and Heber C. Kimball showed up at Joseph's widow's home to give their condolences.[604]

Showing up at Emma Smith's house is the event that took place. We can logically assume that this event took place, because it would be a reasonable act that the highest leaders of the early Mormon Church would visit their prophet's widow to offer their condolences.

A person trying to understand the Real Truth about what happened after Joseph Smith was killed, can reasonably and logically accept that this event is Real Truth.

---

[604] *JS Bio*, 17.

Those who believe that Joseph Smith was a true prophet of God might present their "facts" about Young's and Kimball's visit to the Smith home differently than those who do not believe that he was a prophet of God. Therefore, the Real Truth about the event cannot be confirmed.

But there is an event that is confirmed by both sides. Joseph Smith's wife, Emma Hale Smith; his mother, Lucy Mack Smith; his brother, William Smith; and his closest friends did *not* follow Brigham Young out west and continue Young's version of the religion that had developed among the early LDS/Mormons before the death of their prophet, seer, and revelator.

Shortly after Joseph Smith's murder, his intimates reorganized the Church. It is *logical* and *reasonable* to accept that the Church was in disarray and confusion because their prophet had just been killed. Joseph's family and intimates called it the *Reorganized Church of Jesus Christ of Latter-day Saints*.[605] Meanwhile, Brigham Young

---

[605] *Wikipedia*, "Community of Christ."

and others competed for power and disputed the succession of authority.[606]

From almost the beginning of the religion that was made a legal church (first known as the *Church of Christ,* April 6, 1830), to the day of Joseph's murder, Sidney Rigdon had been Joseph's trusted Counselor in the First Presidency. This *logically* and *reasonably* gave some validity to Rigdon's opposition to Brigham Young.

Both sides of the "Mormon-authorized" "power and priesthood"[607] authority and lineage have their own "facts." Because of this, it is hard to ascertain the *real* reason that Rigdon did not follow Young out west.[608]

Both sides report that when Young and Kimball showed up at Emma's house, her mother-in-law, Lucy Mack, was there consoling her. This seems *logical* and *reasonable.* But only one side reports that Emma kicked

---

[606] *JS Bio*, 18–20, 319, 455 (n. 104). *See also* "Succession crisis (Latter Day Saints)," last modified February 19, 2020, https://en.wikipedia.org/wiki/Succession_crisis_(Latter_Day_Saints).

[607] *See SNS*, 50: "ADAM: 'What is that apron you have on?' ...LUCIFER: 'It is an emblem of my power and Priesthoods.'" *See also JS Bio*, 588–9.

[608] *See JS Bio*, 21.

Young and Kimball out of her house, yelling, "You licentious Fein! Then why not take her sister Mercy?"[609]

It is *logical* and *reasonable* to assume that there were many of Joseph's faithful followers outside of Emma's house wanting to go in and offer their condolences too. This group would later report what Emma said as she was kicking Young and Kimball out of her house.

But the "facts" presented by the side that believes that Young and Kimball were "called by God" to replace Joseph and Hyrum Smith, exclude this event. They do not report what Emma yelled as these two prominent LDS/Mormon leaders exited the door.

It is *logical* and *reasonable* that the LDS/Mormons who believe that Young and Kimball were called of God—in direct opposition of what Joseph's wife, mother, brother, and closest companion believed—would not offer these facts in their history. But this side of the issue (the LDS/Mormon Church) cannot deny that Joseph's intimates did *not* follow

---

[609] *JS Bio*, 17.

Young. Instead, they reorganized the Church in a completely different way than Young did out west in Utah.

Why would Emma Smith call Young or Kimball a "licentious Fein"[610] and call out the name of her sister-in-law, Mercy? An honest reflection of the incident does not determine to which man Emma addressed her remarks.

Keep in mind what *logic* and *reason* is:

Logic deals with the principles and criteria of what one might consider to be true, based on <u>actual</u> events that support what is considered to be true. *Reason* is the ability to determine if the events were *actual.*

Both sides of the issue know that Kimball married Hyrum Smith's widow, Mary Fielding Smith, on September 14, 1844, not even three months after Hyrum's murder.[611] But Hyrum had two wives at the time of his death, one of which was Mary Fielding's sister, Mercy.

---

[610] *JS Bio*, 17.
[611] *JS Bio*, 17.

What could *logically* and *reasonably* be the reason that caused Emma to become so upset that she kicked the men out of her house, yelling, "*You licentious Fein! Then why not take her sister Mercy?*"

Both sides agree that Brigham Young made Heber C. Kimball his right-hand man (First Counselor) in Young's new church in Utah. Both sides agree that both Mary Fielding's son and grandson eventually became leading prophets of Young's Utah church, and that Joseph Smith's descendants had no part of this church. Joseph's son and grandsons became the prophets, seers, and revelators of the *Reorganized Church*.

We (the Real Illuminati™) had no part of either organized church. But we know what happened during the event that took place in Emma's home shortly after the murder of our True Messenger.

A few days before the Smith brothers' murders at Carthage, Illinois, two of Joseph's most trusted friends visited the jail: Dan Jones and William Markham.[612]

---

[612] *JS Bio*, 15.

While incarcerated, Joseph lamented that he was about to be killed. During their discussions, Jones mentioned a prophecy that Joseph had given about the "sealed portion" of the gold plates (from which the *Book of Mormon* had been written).

Joseph had said that if anything ever happened to him, his brother, Hyrum, would assure that the "kingdom of God would roll forth until the Lord accomplished his purposes."[613] This included publishing the sealed portion when the Saints were ready for it.

For this reason, Joseph made his brother an equal to him as the "Assistant President" of the Church in 1841.[614] Jones and Markham asked about this and sought instruction about how Hyrum would proceed if Joseph were killed.

Hyrum took issue with this and said he would give his life for his brother. Nothing else was said until just moments before Hyrum was killed. As bullets flew through the jail cell's door, Hyrum shielded his brother and again

---

[613] *JS Bio*, 307.
[614] *JS Bio*, 344.

reiterated his (Hyrum's) desire to protect Joseph. John Taylor would later report what Joseph said to Hyrum just shortly before that moment:

One day it shall be you who finishes what I could not. May the Lord's work be cut short in the righteousness of what you will do for the Father. I love you my brother, my friend.[615]

A few moments later, a bullet entered Hyrum's face and killed him instantly. Joseph would be killed right after that.

After Brigham Young was notified of Joseph's and Hyrum's murders, he called a meeting of those who were at the jail and asked about the details. Markham and Jones reported what Joseph had said a few days earlier, which left both men confused now: "How could Hyrum fulfill the

[615] *See JS Bio*, 16–17. *See also* Salt Lake City Cemetery, 200 "N" Street, gravesite "Park 14-18-5E," denoting Park Plat, Section 14, Lot 8, Grave 5 East. At this burial plot stands the Hyrum Smith / Christopher Nemelka memorial headstone, erected on June 16, 2010. On the back of that headstone is engraved this prophecy of Joseph Smith spoken to his brother Hyrum in the Carthage, Illinois jail on 27 June 1844, shortly before they were murdered, and in the presence of John Taylor and Willard Richards: "One day it shall be you who finishes what I could not. May the Lord's work be cut short in the righteousness of what you will do for the Father. I love you my brother, my friend."

prophesy that Joseph had given about Hyrum leading the Church, if Hyrum was now dead?"

These concerns were voiced by Markham and Jones to both Emma and to Lucy Mack before they were known by Young. After Markham and Jones had visited Joseph and Hyrum at Carthage on the evening of the 26th, they visited both Emma and Mary Fielding. These men told Emma and Mary the details about what had transpired inside the jail, including what Joseph had said about Hyrum taking his place if anything happened to him.

The revelation of Hyrum taking Josephs' place had made sense to Emma at the time Markham and Jones told her about it. This was because of a blessing that Joseph had recently given to their son, Joseph Smith III. Joseph, Jr. had basically blessed their son to follow in his father's footsteps when he was old enough. Until then, Joseph had explained that Hyrum would tutor and mentor Joseph Smith III until he came of age, if anything were to ever happen to him (to Joseph).

This all took place before Young and Kimball visited Joseph's grieving wife and mother (Emma and Lucy). It didn't take Young too long to invent a solution to the issue at hand, i.e., that Hyrum was no longer living to fulfill the expectations placed upon him. Young announced that it wasn't necessary that Hyrum fulfill the prophesy, as long as one of Hyrum's descendants was still alive and able to.

While visiting with Joseph's wife and mother (Emma and Lucy), Young announced that the Lord had revealed to him that he (Young) was to take care of Emma, and that Heber Kimball was to take care of Mary Fielding. This meant that Emma would become one of Young's plural wives, and that her son would no longer receive her murdered husband's mantle.

Logic and *reason* can easily determine Emma's response. Emma Smith had been very close to Hyrum's first love and wife, Jerusha. While he was married to the love of his life, Hyrum wanted nothing to do with plural marriage, unlike so many other early Mormon men did at the time. After Jerusha's untimely death, Hyrum was the single father of five children. Joseph introduced Mary

Fielding to Hyrum and asked her to help take care of Jerusha's children.

Hyrum could never love Mary like he did Jerusha. A woman can feel these things. Mary knew how special Jerusha's children were to Hyrum. Hyrum married Mary Fielding in December of 1837.[616] For the first while, Hyrum could not have sex with Mary because of his strong love for Jerusha. She was affected by this.

Emma and Jerusha had been best friends. It was hard enough on Mary Fielding to take care of Jerusha's kids, but it was even harder to establish a relationship with her very popular and prominent (in the Church) sister-in-law (Emma). These two women had many problems. However, the mutual death of their husbands brought them together, at least temporarily. Brigham Young's devious plans "received from his god" quickly destroyed their sisterhood and bond.

When Young asked Heber Kimball to step in for Hyrum—take Hyrum's wife and raise Hyrum's kids as his

---

[616] *JS Bio*, 444.

own—Kimball was not shy in telling Young that he was not attracted to Mercy, Hyrum's other wife. Emma could sense this, which led to what she yelled at Kimball as she kicked the two devious men out of her house.

Mary Fielding was elated. She would go on become one of the most popular women in Young's Mormon Church. To further turn the knife in the heart of Emma Smith, none of Hyrum's sons from Jerusha would be given a major role in Young's church. Mary Fielding's son[617] and grandson[618] would each later hold the most coveted position of prophet, seer, and revelator.

As we reveal our involvement in Joseph Smith's life and more of our "great and marvelous work,"[619] *logic* and *reason*, the basis of common sense, will help the reader answer the question that our 1842 play's character, Adam, asks, "How do I know that you are True Messengers?"[620]

---

[617] "Joseph F. Smith," *Wikipedia, The Free Encyclopedia*, last modified February 28, 2020, https://en.wikipedia.org/wiki/Joseph_F._Smith.

[618] "Joseph Fielding Smith," *Wikipedia, The Free Encyclopedia*, last modified March 11, 2020, https://en.wikipedia.org/wiki/Joseph_Fielding_Smith.

[619] *BOM*, 3 Nephi 28:31.

[620] *SNS*, 121.

We can give details that no other person upon Earth knows, not only about Mormonism, but also about the earth itself. We can explain how the earth was in the beginning when all mortals lived upon this planet in equity. In other words, we can give unto you the "sign and token you received in the Garden of Eden."[621]

We can give unto you the "sign and token" of Real Truth—things as they *really* are, as they *really* were, and as they *really* will be in the future. We will give unto you what Christians have sold for money.

Our 1842 play's True Messenger character asks, "Do you sell you signs and tokens for money? You have them I presume."[622] Christians have sold their signs and token for the things of this world. Christians—most prominently the LDS/Mormons who should know better—have taken away and kept back the plain and precious part of the Real Truth ... the Spirit of Christ,[623] given to each mortal upon birth.

---

[621] *SNS*, 121.
[622] *SNS*, 107.
[623] *BOM*, Moroni 7:16.

It is our "great and marvelous work"[624] to teach the world the Real Truth about all things. In this way, the last words of Adam, before he wakes up from *the dream of mortal life* (again, as the god Michael), will be fulfilled:

> These are true messengers. I exhort you to give strict heed to their counsel and teachings, and they will lead you in the way of life and salvation.[625]

Our Adam did NOT say that *Jesus* was going to come back to Earth to "lead you in the way of life and salvation." Our 1842 play clearly stated that Elohim and Jehovah have *nothing to do with* this "lone and dreary world"[626] ... ABSOLUTELY NOTHING.

After our character, Adam, is awakened from the deep sleep, he recognizes that he was a god all along, and that his personal salvation was because of what he knew of the Real Truth.

---

[624] *BOM*, 3 Nephi 28:31.
[625] *SNS*, 123.
[626] *SNS*, 85.

The original last scene, which Brigham Young later removed from our play, presented Michael's last words. After being brought back into the presence of Elohim and Jehovah, and looking directly at the audience, Michael quoted words given by Jesus Christ (Jehovah) from our new American scripture:

> Because ye know these things, ye are redeemed from the fall; therefore ye are brought back into our presence.[627]

Thus was our endowment play presentation presented as the greatest saving ordinance of all.

We are the True Messengers referred to in our play. We explained who we are and how we came to be by allegorical reference in our new American scripture. We are those of whom we wrote, "the Gentiles shall know them not."[628] We have warned the Gentiles about "our words," which are the "words of Jesus":

---

[627] *Compare BOM*, Ether 3:13.
[628] *BOM*, 3 Nephi 28:27–8.

And wo be unto him that will not hearken unto the words of Jesus, **and also to them whom he hath chosen and sent among [the Gentiles]**; for whoso receiveth not the words of Jesus **and the words of those whom he hath sent** receiveth not him; and therefore he will not receive them at the last day; And it would be better for [the Americans] if they had not been born. For do ye suppose that ye can get rid of the justice of an offended God, who hath been trampled under feet of men, that thereby salvation might come?[629]

"That thereby salvation might come"?

Maybe we could have made this particular point clearer in our 1842 play.[630] Before Adam was awakened back into the presence of his True Self (which comprises the Godhead of one's True Self: Elohim, Jehovah, and Michael), perhaps his last words could have been this:

---

[629] *BOM*, 3 Nephi 28:34–5, emphasis added.
[630] *Sacred, not Secret*, https://www.realilluminati.org/sacred-not-secret.

These are true messengers. I exhort you to give strict heed to their counsel and teachings, and they will lead you in the way of life and salvation,[631] because there is no other way that thereby salvation might come. You must save yourselves by listening to these True Messengers.

We are your True Messengers. We are the Real Illuminati™. Listen to us and live.

Reject us, and the prophecies of our new American scripture concerning your rejection will all be fulfilled, both spiritually and temporally.[632]

How could we possibly make our message and intent clearer and more plain and precious?

---

[631] *SNS*, 123.
[632] *BOM*, 1 Nephi 14:7.

Human Enmity

Part Five

Our new American scripture, the *Book of Mormon*, written by us, the Real Illuminati™, has many accounts of wars and violence,[633] culminating in the complete annihilation of two entire races of white-skinned people, the Nephites and the Jaredites.[634]

The book was written for the people of this day. It was not written for people who lived thousands of years ago.

The most popular virtual reality games today (circa 2020) have violent, battle-related themes in which a player can kill other players who are trying to kill them. Males have a natural tendency to fight other males who they believe are a threat to their manhood. In virtual reality games, even the weakest males can choose a game avatar with massive muscles and powerful weapons to destroy

---

[633] "Warfare in the Book of Mormon," *FairMormon*, accessed April 6, 2020, https://www.fairmormon.org/answers/Book_of_Mormon/Warfare.

[634] *BOM*, Ether, chapter 15.

anyone who threatens their manhood. The virtual reality game plays out on the screen and in the mind of the player, who could, in truth, be a physically unattractive and weak male. This is his *hope* of reality.

It was our desire to get people to read the *Book of Mormon*, which included many of the stories that were copied from recorded history. We hoped that the reader would "liken the scriptures unto themselves."[635] We did this by incorporating battle scenes and heroic characters of strength and popularity into our storyline.

We expected our story to reach into the ego of the "natural man."[636] We presented the idea of great warriors and patriots, none of which was as popular as our Captain Moroni.[637] The "natural man" identifies well with this character and is intrigued with the patriotism and military strategy that Moroni uses to win battles. Our efforts to entice the "natural man" to read our book would allow us to give a clue about himself:

---

[635] *BOM*, 2 Nephi 11:2, 8; *see also BOM*, 1 Nephi 19:23–4.
[636] *BOM*, Mosiah 3:19.
[637] *BOM*, Alma 43:16.

For the **natural man is an enemy to God**, and has been from the fall of Adam, and will be, forever and ever, unless he yields to the enticings of the Holy Spirit, and **putteth off the natural man** and becometh a saint through the atonement of Christ the Lord, and becometh as a child, submissive, meek, humble, patient, full of love, willing to submit to all things which the Lord seeth fit to inflict upon him, even as a child doth submit to his father.[638]

Our Captain Moroni character couldn't have been more of a "natural man," an enemy of one's *True Self*.[639] But we needed a hero to whom the "natural men" could relate. This was the reason we included so many wars and battles in our book.[640]

---

[638] *BOM*, Mosiah 3:19, emphasis added.

[639] *See THOR*, 15, 22–3, 241–4 for more information about one's *True Self*.

[640] For a chart of some of the wars and conflicts in the Book of Mormon, *see* BMC Team, "Why are There So Many War Chapters in the Book of Mormon?" *Book of Mormon Central*, August 3, 2016, https://knowhy.bookofmormoncentral.org/knowhy/why-are-there-so-many-war-chapters-in-the-book-of-mormon.

Most of the *Book of Mormon* battles can be traced to those that were recorded in written history, whether the battle was real or fictitious.

For one of many examples, the idea of the "Stripling Warriors," who were young, dark-skinned Lamanites taught by their mothers, came from what was recorded about ancient Greek Spartans. Young Spartans[641] were taught by their mothers until they reached not more than 8 years old. Recruited by the Greek military, these young men were very courageous. "Never had I seen so great courage, nay, not amongst all the [Greeks]."[642]

In our book, we presented an allegory about humanity. We referred to the world as a vineyard and to each person as a branch of an "olive tree."[643] The olive trees were the groups, cultures, and communities of people. The "trees of the vineyard" were planted in various places throughout the vineyard. When several trees were corrupt and did not produce any "good fruit," the Lord of the vineyard and his

---

[641] "The Spartan Family, *HistoryWiz*, accessed March 24, 2020, http://historywiz.com/didyouknow/spartanfamily.htm.

[642] *Compare BOM*, Alma 56:45.

[643] *See BOM*, Jacob, chapter 5.

servants took a branch from the corrupt trees and grafted the branch into a tree growing in a more desirable place in the vineyard. The Lord and his servants pruned, watered, and fertilized the trees with tender care. But regardless of how much care was given to the trees, eventually "none of [the fruit of the trees was] good":[644]

> Behold, I knew that all the fruit of the vineyard, save it were these, had become corrupted. And now these which have once brought forth good fruit have also become corrupted; and now all the trees of my vineyard are good for nothing save it be to be hewn down and cast into the fire.[645]

When the Lord of the vineyard asked his servants what had happened to his vineyard, they responded:

> Is it not the loftiness of thy vineyard—have not the branches thereof overcome the roots which

---

[644] *BOM*, Jacob 5:32.
[645] *BOM*, Jacob 5:42.

are good? And because the branches have overcome the roots thereof, behold they grew faster than the strength of the roots, taking strength unto themselves. Behold, I say, is not this the cause that the trees of thy vineyard have become corrupted?[646]

This "loftiness" (arrogance) is a direct cause of pride. The *roots* of all the "trees of the vineyard" represent the part that makes us human, the part that is not an "enemy of God," but is like "a child, submissive, meek, humble, patient, [and] full of love."[647]

Our roots grew in our early childhood. With these roots, we were as little children before the fruit of our tree became corrupt, before we grew faster than we had strength. But our parents taught us to "take strength unto ourselves," to not take any guff from another, and to become all that we could become. They encouraged us to be the best and most successful that we could be in life,

---

[646] *BOM*, Jacob 5:48.
[647] *BOM*, Mosiah 3:19.

regardless of how our pursuit of success affected others. This was not according to the *roots of our humanity*, but according to the god of this world,[648] *Lucifer* (in other words, human pride and ego).

"Loftiness" (pride and arrogance) is a result of people lacking self-esteem—something each of us possessed in abundance as little children—and then acting out to prove their worth to others.

If someone views another as better than them, they put up an affront (a battle line). There is a natural battle that makes one person dislike another. We do this to protect our self-worth. Everyone wants to feel at least equal to every other person. This social comparison was not part of our childlike humanity; it was not part of our roots. The comparison that creates this dislike (i.e., enmity) is caused by the standards of worth and value that are placed on the individual.

As little children, none of us saw another child as better or worse than us. We had no innate measuring stick

---

[648] *SNS*, Chapter 5, 85–113.

of what is "better" or "worse." These standards and judgments were taught to us.

No little child perceives themselves as poor, until an adult complains about being poor. As a child, we want to please the one from whom we receive, or should receive, unconditional love and acceptance, as well as the necessities of life. So, when our parent complains about their poverty, for example, it is natural for us to want to relieve the burden of our parent.

Instead of accepting our impoverished situation, we learn to fight for a better life. We begin to hate living in poverty. We begin to dislike those who are not living in poverty. This dislike, this enmity, causes us to act out contrary to the roots of our humanity and hate those whom we view act and think like they are better off than we are.

The feeling that we had as a child, of actually being equal with everyone else, does not leave us throughout our life. Every person instinctively feels that he or she is just as good as everyone else. This feeling comes from the Real

Truth that we are all equal advanced humans *playing a virtual reality game* called Mortal Life.[649]

Just as video game players battle each other inside the game to prove their worth, mortals do the same thing anytime they do not feel that life is fair and just.

This feeling of inequity—this enmity for others, who we have been convinced are better than us—will never go away as long as we are "fallen" humans. This *enmity* creates the pride in our Self and also our self-esteem.[650] It is an intricate part of our true reality, for we are all equal advanced human beings.[651]

There will never be peace and goodwill upon Earth until there exists a feeling of *equity* among all people.

We did not write "a feeling of equality" on purpose. "Equity" is the feeling of fairness and impartiality. "Equality" is a state of being equal in all things.

"Equality" upon Earth is not our desire, nor is making everyone equal in all things part of our goals. It has been, is,

---

[649] *See THOR*, Chapter 1.

[650] For further study on "enmity," *see THOR*, 66–8.

[651] *THOR* (large print), 101.

and will always be our goal to make everyone equal, not in <u>all</u> things, but in the basic necessities that are needed in order for a human to live on Earth. This is important from the time a person is born until the time of their death, in order to be able to exercise unabated individual free will.

We (Real Illuminati™) have no desire for *equality* with the minority. We have no desire to be *equal* with those who are seen by the world as wealthy, popular, and successful, or as knowledgeable and wise. For this reason, our identities are always kept secret, none of us wanting any credit for what we know and what we do.

At times, we have pretended to be "simple and illiterate" so that we could infiltrate the collusions (secret combinations) and plans of those in power. This was not done to take away their power or designs, but in hopes of influencing a different, more *equitable design* for those affected by their wealth and power. It has always been done in an effort "to control them without dominating them."

We have explained how we operate according to this manner in our first book, *The True History of Religion*.[652]

There are many people on Earth who have no desire to be *equally* wealthy or popular with the few. But ALL people want to believe that they have a fair and impartial opportunity to *become* equally wealthy, if they so choose.

All people on Earth desire to be treated with fairness and impartiality (with independence of free will, not influenced by a particular person or group). All people on Earth want *equity*. This desire comes because deep in our hearts we DO feel *equal* with everyone else. When another person controls our life and forces us to do something that we don't want to do, we do not feel that we are being treated fairly and impartially—where *impartiality* means the ability to exercise individual unconditional free will.

A person does not feel it is *equitable* (fair and impartial) when there are those in this world who can do what they want, when they want, if they want, while others cannot. If life upon Earth allowed each person to be free to

---

[652] *THOR* (large print), 274–8.

do what each wants, when each wants, if each wants, then *equity* would exist. Because there are no two humans who are alike, and each has different desires that make them happy, *equality* doesn't really matter; but *equity* does.

Perhaps a person is happy sitting at home, writing music, and playing an instrument. Being forced to work most of their waking hours at something they don't want to do so that they can earn money for food, clothing, shelter, or healthcare, feels unfair and unjust.

This feeling would not exist IF there were **no** humans who did what they wanted to do, when they wanted to do it, if they chose to do it. Because there are those who have more freedom because of their particular economic advantage, the disadvantaged will always feel unfairly treated.

IF it were impossible for a person living on Earth to become wealthy and powerful, thus allowing the person unconditional free will, then there wouldn't exist a feeling of unfairness. In other words, if all humans suffered equally and none could do what they wanted, then we would all feel united in our common fate and none would feel slighted. But this is not the case.

In these current times, humans cannot live without the basic requirements that the laws of nature's earth demands. Our bodies are made from elements of this earth; thus they require the same elements of the earth to sustain the body.

Further, our current world spins in an order that creates weather conditions that are not suitable for our current bodies. There are parts of Earth where humans can live year-round without clothing or shelter to protect from the weather. But these places are the exception and not the rule of the current environment.

Planet Earth has not always been the way that it is today. Humans didn't always have the type of physical bodies that we have now.[653] Earth did not always spin in the course of its current order, creating unsuitable climates and conditions (hurricanes, tornados, volcanos, earthquakes, etc.). We can prove this with logic and reason.

---

[653] *THOR* (large print), 19–20.

Let's suppose that we advanced many years into the future and have figured out how to create the perfect planet for human habitation. We would want to have the ability to create it in such a way that it spins in space in an ordered pattern that we have preprogrammed that provides the best results for humanity. This would allow us to keep the majority of our new planet always facing the sun. Thus, it would receive from the sun the precise energy that would create the perfect human climate.

If we had the ability, what kind of human body would we create for this perfect world? Today, humans are discovering ways to manipulate genes (DNA) and engineer them to do what humans want. Soon, if religion and the ignorance it causes does not intervene and stop progress, humans will be able to create a new type of human body. We will be able to create one that doesn't get sick or age, one that has its own energy source so that it doesn't need food ... even one that does not need oxygen.

The only thing that is standing in the way of this type of scientific discovery and progression is religion.

Regardless of the human potential in creating a great world for ALL under the rule of *equity*, religion is needed and will always be needed, as long as people do not feel equity with others.

Understanding how the brain can become its own energy source is as easy as understanding how an atom can create powerful nuclear energy. It is called "nuclear" energy because the energy is generated from the *nucleus* of an atom.

The human brain is made up of atoms. Advanced technology will be able to create a brain that has its own cerebral nuclear reactor that provides the body with energy. A human body can be created that replaces the circulatory system by enhancing the nervous system. Instead of blood supplying the body with nutrients, nerves will replace capillaries, veins, arteries, and other blood-carrying vessels and supply the body with *nuclear* energy produced in the brain's own reactor.

Along with this advanced type of body's ability to create its own energy, its brain will have its own thermostat that delivers needed energy to any part of the body that requires warmth or cooling.

Furthermore, and most importantly, this perfect body's energy source (brain) could create a magnetic field that prohibits any other atom from touching the atoms of which the body is created. This would be a powerful force field that could not be penetrated by anything in the universe. It would protect the individual from being physically hurt. The person's brain would control when to turn off the magnetic force field in order to allow energy from the environment to enter through the human senses of sight, smell, taste, sound, and touch. If the perfect human didn't want to see something, they wouldn't see it. If the perfect human didn't want to smell something, they wouldn't smell it ... and so forth.

We bring these things to your attention because we know that this Earth was once the perfect place for humans to exist. We know that the first humans placed upon this planet had these perfect types of bodies that functioned as we have described them above. This is what we referred to when we used the idea of a "Garden of Eden," before the "fall"[654] of humankind, in our efforts to influence the religious mind.

As we explained above,

The only thing that is standing in the way of this type of scientific discovery and progression is religion.

We have mentioned the above perfect human existence because it makes sense to all logical-thinking people, that if humanity were to progress many thousands of years into the future, this *could* be possible.

We, the Real Illuminati™, know these things are possible because we know why and how planet Earth exists.

(Although we touch upon these Real Truths at times to make a point, we will not delve into them at this time. In the future, if humanity responds sufficiently to our message, we will provide more details in our final warning to the human race: *The Dream of Mortal Life,*

---

[654] *SNS*, Chapter 3.

Understanding Human Reality—A Final Warning to the Human Race, a free book.)[655]

Religion is not the cause of humanity's sickness. Religion is a drug that treats a symptom of this sickness. The sickness is *inequity*. Religion makes the "least among [us]"[656] feel just as special in "God's" eyes as those who are seen as the "greatest among us."[657]

Religion counters the affliction and control that those who seem to be prospering in life create in the mind of the "least." The belief that the god that created all humankind sees all of his children as equals offsets the feeling of inferiority and struggle that the majority sees and feels.

In the minds of the poor and afflicted, God condemns the rich for what they have done and will punish them in heaven. In the minds of the rich, God has blessed them with riches and prosperity.

---

[655] "The Dream of Mortal Life," *Real Illuminati*™, accessed March 29, 2020, https://www.realilluminati.org/dream-of-mortal-life.

[656] Luke 9:48.

[657] *See* Luke 9:48.

On September 11, 2001, Allah, the god of Islam,[658] brought to heaven and rewarded nineteen of His faithful followers for punishing the wealthy nation that was responsible for the suffering and *inequity* of Allah's chosen people.[659] It was the Spirit of God (Allah) that inspired these nineteen men to sacrifice their lives. This was done to punish the "infidels" responsible for the poverty and affliction of Allah's children living in the land that Allah gave to their ancestors many years ago.

This was the very reason why the Twin Towers and the Pentagon (the world's economic center and the U.S. military command center) were attacked.[660] These buildings represented those responsible, according to the Spirit of Allah[661] in each of these nineteen men, for the economic

---

[658] Asma Afsaruddin, "Allah," *Encyclopedia Britannica*, last modified September 16, 2019, https://www.britannica.com/topic/Allah.

[659] "September 11 attacks," *Wikipedia, The Free Encyclopedia*, last modified March 21, 2020, https://en.wikipedia.org/wiki/September_11_attacks.

[660] Contrast this Real Truth *with* "Motives for the September 11 attacks, *Wikipedia, The Free Encyclopedia*, last modified April 5, 2020, https://en.wikipedia.org/wiki/Motives_for_the_September_11_attacks.

[661] "God in Islam," *Wikipedia, The Free Encyclopedia*, last modified April 4, 2020, https://en.wikipedia.org/wiki/God_in_Islam.

instability (caused by the Twin Towers) and physical affliction (caused by the U.S. military) of the Muslim people.

Pride is our common enemy.

Pride is responsible for all human misery. Pride is the cause of the economic disparity (differences) that exists. Pride is why we join religious groups or movements. Pride is why we are attracted to separate families, communities, and nations. Pride is why humans "reign with blood and horror on the earth."[662]

Eliminating pride from the human demeanor seems impossible. Pride burdens us—"bruises our heals"[663]—as we walk along the path of life in this "lone and dreary world";[664] but we do have the power to "crush its head."[665] In order to crush pride's head, which is actually the source (the head) from where pride's energy originated, we must understand exactly what pride is and where it comes from.

Unlike any other life form in the Universe, humans have a conscience that makes them feel badly when they

---

[662] *SNS*, 59.
[663] *SNS*, 58.
[664] *SNS*, 85.
[665] *SNS*, 58.

do something bad, and good, when they do something good. When we behave in ways that don't support the humane alignment of our conscience, we feel a dislike (enmity) towards the action. And nothing feels worse to us than unfairness and injustice … two words that only humans can comprehend.

As mentioned above, the "terrorists" felt *enmity* that the United States was treating them, their families, their communities, and their religion unfairly and unjustly. It was their "pride" that took this *enmity* and "reigned with blood and horror"[666] upon the people of the United States.[667]

We knew that the European immigrants *planted* in the "North American part of the vineyard" were very prideful and arrogant about their new land and government. These *American branches* "grew faster than the strength of the roots, taking strength unto themselves."[668]

We provided clues to this when we had Joseph Smith, Jr. present a play to a few of his close associates on May 4,

---

[666] *SNS*, 58.
[667] *Wikipedia*, "September 11 attacks."
[668] *BOM*, Jacob 5:48.

1842 in Nauvoo, Illinois. The play's dress rehearsal included dressing the character playing Lucifer[669] in the same type of masonic apron worn by George Washington and other Freemasons in attendance at the U.S. Capitol's cornerstone-laying ceremony.[670] Besides using the same clothing worn by the Freemasons, Joseph's play incorporated many of the same secret signs and tokens they used.

It was our intent to show that the early American people were following *Lucifer* (their natural pride and ego) and that their government was set up and being influenced by human pride and ego. This is why we instructed Joseph Smith to dress Lucifer's character in Freemason regalia (ceremonial dress) and use their symbols.

What Mormons have never understood is that Joseph did not act until he received counsel from us (the Real

---

[669] The first person to play the part of *Lucifer* was William Law. Law was a Second Counselor in the First Presidency of the LDS/Mormon Church at that time and later turned on Joseph. He was one of the main perpetrators involved in Joseph Smith's eventual murder. Law used American justice supporting freedom of speech and of the press to create his own newspaper called the *Nauvoo Expositor*. Law railed on Joseph Smith and the policies that Law believed Joseph had created and espoused. He especially criticized the idea of polygamy, a religious doctrine that Joseph Smith Jr. did not promote or support, opposite of his successor, Brigham Young, who later did. (*See JS Bio*, Appendix 2.)

[670] Committee on Masonic Education, "Masonic Questions & Answers," *subtopic* "American Masonic History," *Grand Lodge of Pennsylvania*, accessed March 29, 2020, https://pagrandlodge.org/masonic-q-and-a/.

Illuminati™) first. This was not a play written by Joseph Smith, Jr. We were its playwrights.

Our play was meant to be allegorical in nature, presenting the "mysteries of God [in full] ... according to the portion of his word which he doth grant unto the children of men, according to the heed and diligence which they give unto him."[671]

The early European-American Christians had the Bible, the "portion of his word which [they believed God granted] unto the children of men,"[672] which is the only thing to which they gave heed and diligence. So we used the religious ideologies from the popular King James Bible to create our play's allegories. We utilized the Freemasons' pride and secret institution to present the workings of *Lucifer* and the development of the United States of America.

We developed this play after the pattern of the ancient Greeks.[673] These were the first people in this earth's

---

[671] *See BOM*, Alma 12:9–11.

[672] *BOM*, Alma 9:10.

[673] Mark Cartwright, "Ancient Greek Theatre," *Ancient History Encyclopedia*, July 14, 2016, https://www.ancient.eu/Greek_Theatre/.

current "dispensation of time"[674] to write and perform plays (circa 500 BCE). Adroit Greek playwrights developed six parts to a play's presentation: (1) Plot, (2) Characters, (3) Theme, (4) Dialogue, (5) Rhythm, and (6) Spectacle.[675]

The plot is the chain of events that advances the play's narrative (story) by presenting appropriate themes for each scene or act. Characters are included to explain the story and provide the audience with an opportunity to personally identify with those characters created to present the plot. The characters are woven into the storyline so that when the characters speak their lines, the narrative becomes personal to each member of the audience. The tempo (rhythm) and spectacle of the play keep the audience's attention.

The first scene of our play introduces its theme, along with the first three main characters. The plot is the Real Truth about human existence. The first scene presents the

---

[674] Each dispensation of time represents a period when there existed global human cooperation. *See also THOR* (large print), 21–2.

[675] *Compare* Bonnie Hoffman, "Six Aristotelian Elements of a Play," *Bellevue College*, accessed April 4, 2020, https://www2.bellevuecollege.edu/artshum/materials/drama/Hoffman/101SIXARISTOAPLAYspr03.asp.

creation of the world and of humankind by those perceived as the Christian Godhead: the Father (Elohim), the Son (Jehovah), and the Holy Ghost (Michael).

The acts and scenes that follow, support the theme and introduce other characters who help to produce a climatic ending. The final act (denouement)[676] of our original script draws together all of the other acts and explains a Real Truth about human existence and consciousness that was rarely considered before we presented our play:

All humans upon Earth are equal, highly advanced human beings experiencing a dream sequence of events that their dream Self recognizes as their mortal life.

The first scene of our play presents the equal gods: Elohim, Jehovah, and Michael, creating the earth. Once

---

[676] Definition: "the final outcome of the main dramatic complication in a literary work." *See* "denouement," in *Merriam-Webster Dictionary*, accessed April 4, 2020, https://www.merriam-webster.com/dictionary/denouement.

Earth's environment is created and the plants and animals are placed upon it by the gods—"like unto the worlds that we have heretofore formed"—the gods contemplate the existence of mortal humankind on Earth:[677]

ELOHIM: Jehovah, Michael, is man found upon the earth?

JEHOVAH: Man is not found on the earth, Elohim.

[MICHAEL: That is correct. Man is not found on the earth, Elohim.]

ELOHIM: Jehovah, Michael, then let us go down and form man in our own likeness and in our own image, male and female, and put into him his spirit, and let us give him dominion over the beasts, the fishes, and the birds, and make him lord over the earth, and over all things on the face of the earth. We will plant for him a garden, eastward in Eden, and place him in it to tend and cultivate it, that he may be happy and have joy

---

[677] *SNS*, 20.

therein. We will command him to multiply and replenish the earth, that he may have joy and rejoicing in his posterity. We will place before him the Tree of Knowledge of Good and Evil, and we will allow Lucifer, our common enemy, whom we shall also place upon the earth, and whom we have thrust out, to tempt him, and to try him, that he may know by his own experience the good from the evil. If he yields to the temptation of Lucifer, we will give unto him The Law of Sacrifice, and we will provide a Savior for him, as we counseled in the beginning, that man may be brought forth by the power of the redemption and the resurrection, and come again into our presence, and with us partake of Eternal Life and exaltation. We will call this the Sixth Day, and we will rest from our labors for a season. Come; let us go down.[678]

---

[678] *SNS*, 31.

In order to create mortal kind on Earth, the god Michael is put to sleep and awakens in a dream state, in which he no longer recognizes himself as a god equal to Elohim and Jehovah. Not remembering anything before his "birth" (creation) on Earth, Michael is called "Adam." The characters "Eve" and "Lucifer" are then introduced on stage.

Explained according to modern psychoanalysis (therapy), our play's sub-characters, Adam, Eve, and Lucifer, represent respectively, the Superego, the Ego, and the Id. Likewise, the characters Elohim, Jehovah, and Michael represent parts of our human True Advanced Self.

Elohim represents the power and control one has over one's own existence. *Jehovah* represents the individual sense of right and wrong (the judgment factor of our conscience). And *Michael* represents our individual free will to make choices with one's power and control over the Self.

All of these characters combine to represent parts of the Self, both advanced and mortal. We presented this Real Truth allegorically, according to what our intended religiously oriented audience would not automatically dismiss, with references and similarities to the Bible.

In our play, we clearly present mortal kind (Adam, Eve, and Lucifer) as existing in a "lone and dreary world,"[679] without the participation of, or involvement with, Elohim or Jehovah.

The only source of inspiration, revelation, divinity, or any other kind of emotional stimulus often associated with God, is the "god of this world," i.e., *Lucifer*.[680] This point is undeniable in our presentation. It was meant to explain that all religion upon Earth, all scripture "mingled with the philosophies of men,"[681] and everything associated with "God," was and is the result of our fallen nature's pride and ego—our common enemy.

This natural man, or woman, is *Lucifer*, the "common enemy"[682] of our True Selves—our personal pride and ego.

---

[679] *SNS*, 85.
[680] *SNS*, Chapter 5, 85–113.
[681] *Compare SNS*, 87.
[682] *SNS*, 31.

Our play's character, Lucifer, was meant to represent only this ... nothing more and nothing less.

According to Bible stories, Adam fell in the Garden of Eden after being tempted by Lucifer.[683] As we presented in our original script, Lucifer was just as much a part of Adam, as was Eve. Lucifer did not appear until the god Michael was put to sleep and began to dream.[684]

After the "fall of humankind," represented by the characters Adam and Eve partaking of the forbidden fruit in the Garden of Eden, our character Elohim confronts Adam and Eve about what they have done:

ELOHIM: Eve! What is this that thou hast done?

EVE: The serpent beguiled me, and I did eat.

ELOHIM: Lucifer! What hast thou been doing here?

LUCIFER: I have been doing that which has been done in other worlds.

ELOHIM: What is that?

LUCIFER: I have been giving some of the fruit of the Tree of the Knowledge of Good and Evil to them.

ELOHIM: Lucifer, because thou hast done this, thou shalt be cursed above all the beasts of the field. Upon thy belly thou shalt go, and dust shalt thou eat all the days of thy life.[685]

Keep in mind that our character Lucifer represents human pride. Pride affects our ego (ego is represented by Eve) and causes us to do behaviors or actions that we might not otherwise do according to the innate alignment of our humane Self.

This eternal alignment (which we all have in common) is the Superego that is represented by our character Adam. Our pride (which we all have in common too) tries to get us to behave in ways that don't feel right according to the humane alignment of our conscience. (This is why Adam is tempted by Lucifer in our play.)

---

[685] *SNS*, 55–7.

Remember, in our play, Adam represents the *god Michael*, asleep and acting and being acted upon in a dream experience.[686] The characters *Elohim* and *Jehovah* represent the other two parts of Adam's True Self—his *true nature*.

When our pride tries to get us to do something that is not in line with our *true nature* (which is "the Father" in our symbolic presentation), our Superego's immediate response is this (again according to our allegorical play):

I will not partake of that fruit [do that thing]. Father told me [my conscience tells me] that in the day I should partake of it I should surely die [fall from my true nature].[687]

Once mortals give in to their pride (the enticements of the flesh) in mortality, they are led by their worldly appetites and the desires of the flesh ("Upon thy belly

---

[686] *SNS*, 35–6.
[687] *SNS*, 45.

thou shalt go").[688] However, their worldly appetite (belly) will never be satisfied following their pride. The "food" that they eat is of the "dust" of the earth[689] (the things of this world).

"For dust thou art and unto dust thou shalt return,"[690] actually means that nothing we do while in the flesh is of any consequence or worth once we are no longer in the flesh.

When a person walks along a path *made of dust*, they raise up dust. This "dust" has no nutritional value whatsoever. This person will continually be "eating" in an attempt to satisfy the "belly" upon which they proceed throughout life, but will never feel satisfied or fulfilled.

In order to feel satiated, or better, completely happy, a human must act according to their own conscience, which has been explained above.

As we "eat the dust of the earth,"[691] we never connect with who we really are and find lasting happiness ... we never align our conscience with our Higher Self. We fail

---

[688] *SNS*, 57.
[689] *SNS*, 57.
[690] *Compare* Genesis 3:19.
[691] *Compare SNS*, 57.

because we often follow a dusty path carved in the Earth by those who have the same limited brain capacity as we do.

These people likewise fail to live in equity according to their innate human conscience. When we do not live up to our unique (compared to all other animals) human nature, we feel ENMITY (discomfort) for what we are doing or what is being done to us.

Our 1842 play continues:

LUCIFER: If thou cursest me for doing the same thing which has been done in other worlds, I will take the spirits that follow me, and they shall possess the bodies thou createst for Adam and Eve!

ELOHIM: I will place enmity between thee and the seed of the woman. Thou mayest have power to bruise his heel, but he shall have power to crush thy head.

LUCIFER: Then with that enmity I will take the treasures of the earth, and with gold and silver I will buy up armies and navies, popes and priests, and reign with blood and horror on the earth![692]

Each of us has an innate, deep part of the human soul that makes each of us feel just as good, important, and capable as everyone else. We feel we are of the same worth as everyone else in the world. This is our mutually shared alignment that we allegorically associated with our character Elohim (the true nature of our True Self). It is responsible for all human misery. It is Elohim that places this enmity (discomfort).[693]

Our "common enemy"[694] is pride, the part of us that wants to become like those whom we *perceive* are better than us. In our play, we represent this by Adam not remembering that he is actually equal with Elohim and Jehovah. He feels like he *should be*, at least that's what his

---

[692] *SNS*, 58–9, underlining added.

[693] The feeling of inequity, a battle for self-worth in comparison with others. *See page* 285: "There is a natural battle that makes one person dislike another. We do this to protect our self-worth. Everyone wants to feel at least equal to every other person. This social comparison was not part of our childlike humanity; it was not part of our roots. The comparison that creates this dislike (i.e. enmity) is caused by the standards of worth and value that are placed on the individual."

[694] *SNS*, 31.

inner alignment (still small voice) whispers to him. Not feeling like he is equal to Elohim and Jehovah, Adam is tempted by his pride (Lucifer). But it is Adam's mortal ego (Eve) that is convinced by his pride.

> PRIDE: EGO, here is some of the fruit of that tree. It will make you wise. It is delicious to the taste, and very desirable.
>
> EGO: Who are you?
>
> PRIDE: I am your brother [*i.e., a natural part of you*].
>
> EGO: You, my brother, and come here to persuade me to disobey Father?
>
> PRIDE: I have said nothing about Father. I want you to eat of the fruit of the Tree of Knowledge of Good and Evil, that your eyes may be opened; for that is the way Father gained His knowledge [*that is the way that you will become equal with Elohim ... that is the way that you can align your conscience with your true nature*]. You must eat of this fruit so as to comprehend that everything

has its opposite: good and evil, virtue and vice, light and darkness, health and sickness, pleasure and pain; and thus your eyes will be opened and you will have knowledge.

EGO: Is there no other way?

PRIDE: There is no other way.

EGO: Then I will partake *[go against the alignment of my true nature and do something I know is wrong].*[695]

In our play, the characters Elohim, Jehovah, and Michael said that they were going to allow:

Lucifer, our common enemy, whom we shall also place upon the earth and whom we have thrust out, to tempt [Adam], and to try him, that he may know by his own experience the good from the evil.[696]

---

[695] *Compare SNS*, 46.
[696] *SNS*, 31.

Pride and ego can play no part in a perfect human world where all people are equal. We presented this concept by stating that pride has been "thrust out"[697] by our True Self's—Elohim, Jehovah, and Michael, the three parts that represent the makeup of our True Self—our eternal human nature.

Our "common enemy"[698] is the feeling that we are not as good as everyone else. It is "common" because we ARE as good as everyone else, but have been convinced by our mortal experiences that we are not.

None of us likes to be around a proud person who thinks that he or she is better than we are. We dislike it. It is felt as *enmity* to our conscience. We feel discomfort because the Real Truth is that we are all equal advanced human beings. Our conscience reminds us of that.

PRIDE: Then with that enmity I will take the treasures of the earth, and with gold and silver I

---

[697] *SNS*, 31.
[698] *SNS*, 31.

will buy up armies and navies, popes and priests, and reign with blood and horror on the earth![699]

Our pride makes us want to make more money than others. Our pride attracts us to "popes and priests,"[700] because we believe that these men have priesthood power that makes them better than us. But if they offer us some of their pretended "power of God"[701] through priesthood appointments and offices, we *buy into it* (through tithes and offerings … "with gold and silver")[702] and it comforts our feelings of inequity.

As we explained in the first book of our Trilogy, *The True History of Religion*, all religions started with a person, usually a man, not feeling equal with other men.[703] If a not-so-attractive man can convince a woman that he has priesthood authority (the power to act in God's name), his

[699] *Compare SNS*, 59.
[700] *SNS*, 59.
[701] *BOM*, 1 Nephi 13:18–19, 30.
[702] *See* "Online Donations—United States," *The Church of Jesus Christ of Latter-day Saints*, January 7, 2020, https://www.churchofjesuschrist.org/help/support/finance/online-donations.
[703] *THOR*, 63.

feeling of inequality to more attractive men is compensated for with a sense of equality.

If a man has a gun, he feels as strong as any other man in the world, and even stronger than men who don't have a gun. A man's pride is augmented and supported by both priesthood authority (popes and priests) and guns (armies and navies).[704] It is human pride and ego that makes it worthwhile for many to play virtual video games of "blood and horror."

If the Real Truth were known, mortals would understand that mortal life is nothing more and nothing less than a virtual game. It is being played out like it is because of our "common enemy"[705] that has caused our world to fall from what it was like in the beginning.[706] But these are "mysteries of God."[707] This is the Real Truth.

One can only imagine what would have happened to Joseph Smith had he plainly taught the people that there was no real god.

[704] *SNS*, 59–60.
[705] *SNS*, 31.
[706] *THOR*, 20–1.
[707] *BOM*, Alma 12:9; 26:22; 1 Nephi 10:19; Mosiah 2:9.

How would early American Christians have reacted to the Real Truth that all religion, all inspiration, all answers to all religious prayers (regardless of the manner or any degree of sincerity in which prayers are given), are only heard and answered by a person's own pride and ego?

Throughout his life, Joseph Smith often told his followers that if he were to tell them everything that he knew about the mysteries of God (i.e., the Real Truth), they would "rise up and kill [him]."[708]

There was no Mormon (member of the Church of Jesus Christ of Latter-day Saints), or anyone else for that matter, upon Earth who ever came to understand the "mysteries of God in full."[709] They did not understand in Joseph's day and they do not understand today.

We made it perfectly clear in our play presentation, as well as in our new scripture (the *Book of Mormon*), that if one did not understand the "mysteries of God in full,"[710] one would be under the power and influence of *Lucifer*

---

[708] "Reminiscences of the Church in Nauvoo," 585.

[709] *See BOM*, Alma 12:10.

[710] *See BOM*, Alma 12:10.

(the character in our play that we costumed in the Masonic apron):

It is given unto many to know the mysteries of God; nevertheless they are laid under a strict command that they shall not impart only according to the portion of his word which he doth grant unto the children of men, according to the heed and diligence which they give unto him.

And therefore, he that will harden his heart, the same receiveth the lesser portion of the word; and he that will not harden his heart, to him is given the greater portion of the word, until it is given unto him to know the mysteries of God until he know them in full.

And they that will harden their hearts, to them is given the lesser portion of the word until they know nothing concerning his mysteries; and then they are taken captive by the devil, and led by his will down to destruction. Now this is what is meant by the chains of hell.[711]

Our denouement (final scene) is what culminated and tied together the overall plot of our play.

The original final scene proves unequivocally that the LDS/Mormon people—those who belong to the organized religion formed by misuse and misinterpretation of our play and our new American scripture—are far from latter-day "Saints."[712]

They are greatly deceived and are taken captive by [their pride and ego], and led by [the will of their pride and ego] "down to destruction. Now this is what is meant by the chains of hell."[713] They know nothing of the mysteries of God, and certainly do not know these mysteries "in full."[714]

---

[711] *BOM*, Alma 12:9–11.
[712] *BOM*, Mosiah 3:19.
[713] *BOM*, Alma 12:11.
[714] *BOM*, Alma 12:10.

The people who viewed our original play were confused by its ending. In our original script, the final scene showed the gods, Elohim and Jehovah, standing behind a chair in which was seated the god Michael with his head down, still asleep. They woke Michael up. After Michael said a few important words to the audience, our play ended.

The confusion among the audience was, "What happened to Adam, Eve, and Lucifer?"

After Joseph Smith Jr. was murdered, Brigham Young took control of the LDS/Mormon Church. Brigham Young had no choice but to remove the denouement of our original play, because the Mormons could not understand it and Young could not properly explain its meaning to his followers.

The early followers of Mormonism (the religious movement that followed the publication of our book in 1830) did not understand the symbolism and allegory behind the script we wrote for the play. This ignorance (blindness and deafness in *seeing* and *hearing*)[715] prevented the Mormons from understanding what our script was trying to teach them.

Our play was eventually turned into what would become known as the "temple endowment ceremony."[716] Although changed many times from its original presentation,[717] our play, as subsequently modified by LDS/Mormon leaders, would eventually become the most sacred and desired ordinance of one of the wealthiest religion on Earth: the LDS/Mormon Church (the Church of Jesus Christ of Latter-day Saints).[718]

Mormons are not the only ones who suffer from pride. It was (and is) the pride and arrogance of the American people that keep them in chains of ignorance as well.

The United States grew faster than ever imagined by its Founders. Thomas Jefferson claimed that it would take

---

[715] Isaiah 42:18–19.

[716] "Temple Endowment," *The Church of Jesus Christ of Latter-day Saints*.

[717] "Timeline," http://www.ldsendowment.org/timeline.html. For a recent report on changes, *see* Peggy Fletcher Stack and David Noyce, "LDS Church changes temple ceremony; faithful feminists will see revisions and additions as a 'leap forward'," *The Salt Lake Tribune*, January 3, 2019, https://www.sltrib.com/religion/2019/01/02/lds-church-releases/.

[718] *Wikipedia*, "List of wealthiest organizations."

over 1000 years for the Americans to settle the West (land west of the Mississippi); it took them less than 100 years.

The Americans "grew faster than the strength of [their humanity], taking strength unto themselves."[719]

With little regard for the native American inhabitants, we saw how fast the European "branches" were producing all kinds of fruit, all of which was "bad fruit." This was one of the reasons why we wrote our new American scripture (the *Book of Mormon*).

We wrote the *Book of Mormon* as a countermeasure to human pride, a result of the fallen nature of humans living upon Earth. We can refer to mortal "fallen"[720] nature as that which has created a world that is not equitable for all humans.

But there is only one thing that can truly "crush [the] head"[721] of human pride. There is only thing that can truly "[redeem us] from the fall":[722]

---

[719] *BOM*, Jacob, chapter 5.
[720] *BOM*, Mosiah 16:4.
[721] *SNS*, 58.
[722] *BOM*, Ether 3:13.

KNOWLEDGE OF REAL TRUTH, HOW THINGS REALLY
ARE AND HOW THINGS REALLY WERE IN THE PAST.

This knowledge of Real Truth can determine the future for humanity.

We tried to make this perfectly clear in our new scripture. When we wrote the story of the Jaredites, we purposefully explained how we "are [actually] redeemed from the fall":

Because thou knowest these things ye are redeemed from the fall; therefore ye are brought back into my presence.[723]

Throughout our new scripture, we explained that all mortals are under the grasp and control of *Lucifer* (pride), and will be forever and ever, UNTIL they know the "mysteries of God in full."[724]

---

[723] *BOM*, Ether 3:13.
[724] *BOM*, Alma 12:9–11.

Humanity cannot be saved without the knowledge of what needs to be done to save us. No god, no priesthood, no religion, has ever done anything but "reign with blood and horror upon this earth."[725]

Humans have the power to "crush [pride's] head."[726] But it cannot be done without knowing Real Truth.

Before humanity can be saved, humans must be convinced where the true source of salvation comes. Humans must be convinced that there is no god outside of their own minds. The only way humanity will be saved is if humanity saves itself.

We presented the idea of a *False* and *True Order of Prayer* in our 1842 play.[727] The former (*False Order of Prayer*) is what all religious people do, which is words coming out of their mouth to a god that they cannot see. Nor does the god to which they pray exist. When engaged in this *False Order of Prayer,* the world is deceived by human pride and ego.

---

[725] *SNS,* 59.
[726] *SNS,* 58.
[727] *Sacred, not Secret,* https://www.realilluminati.org/sacred-not-secret.

The *True Order of Prayer* is not any words. It is action. It is the way that humans form a perfect circle of unity, equity, and the greatest binding emotion of all: love. It is the way that we support each other and form a bond between us that is strong.

Humanity can only be saved through an understanding of things as they *really* are and as they *really* were in the past. This is the Real Truth. Understanding the Real Truth today, and learning from the past, we have the power to crush the head of human pride and ego and unite ourselves in such a way that will benefit the whole of humanity.

Religion is the false "philosophies of men mingled with scripture."[728] It has deceived the world. It controls the world. It gives humanity a false hope in something that is actually causing humanity's demise.

Let us help you become part of the solution. Let us help you crush what has bruised humanity's heel as we all walk along the path of life. Grab on to what we know. Hold fast to our rod of iron, and we will lead you to the *Tree of Life.*[729]

---

[728] *SNS*, 87.
[729] *BOM*, 1 Nephi 11:25.

If not, we will deliver you to the hardness of your hearts and the blindness of your minds, which will inevitably lead to your destruction, both temporally and spiritually.[730]

The "philosophies of men mingled with scripture,"[731] are responsible for the religions that entice, encourage, and support the natural enemy of all of humanity: pride and ego ... *Lucifer*, the god of this world.[732] We had no other intent besides inventing and introducing a *new perspective* about these philosophies of men mingled with scripture.

For this purpose we wrote a new American scripture (the *Book of Mormon*).[733]

---

[730] 1 Nephi 14:7.

[731] *JS Bio*, 24–5, 106, 207, 242, 293. *See also SNS*, 87, 105.

[732] *SNS*, Chapter 5, 85–113.

[733] "Book of Mormon," https://www.realilluminati.org/the-book-of-mormon.

Bibliography

"5 Richest Religious Organizations In The World." *2 Minute Facts*. Accessed April 3, 2020. https://2minutefacts.com/5-richest-religious-organizations-in-the-world/.

"A New American Scripture." *Real Illuminati™*. Accessed March 29, 2020. https://www.realilluminati.org/a-new-american-scripture-u1xei.

"About the Temple Endowment." *The Church of Jesus Christ of Latter-day Saints*. Accessed April 5, 2020. https://www.churchofjesuschrist.org/temples/what-is-temple-endowment.

"About Us—The Real Illuminati™." *Real Illuminati™*. Accessed March 29, 2020. https://www.realilluminati.org/about-us.

"Adolf Hitler." *Wikipedia, The Free Encyclopedia*. Last modified March 29, 2020. https://en.wikipedia.org/wiki/Adolf_Hitler.

"American Dream." *Wikipedia, The Free Encyclopedia*. Last modified March 15, 2020. https://en.wikipedia.org/wiki/American_Dream.

"Articles of Confederation." *Wikipedia, The Free Encyclopedia*. Last modified March 19, 2020. https://en.wikipedia.org/wiki/Articles_of_Confederation.

"Atacama Desert." *Wikipedia, The Free Encyclopedia*. Last modified March 29, 2020. https://en.wikipedia.org/wiki/Atacama_Desert.

"Babylonian captivity." *Encyclopedia Britannica*. Last modified April 9, 2019. https://www.britannica.com/event/Babylonian-Captivity.

"Babylonian captivity." *Wikipedia, The Free Encyclopedia*. Last modified April 3, 2020. https://en.wikipedia.org/wiki/Babylonian_captivity.

"Background surrounding the 1990 changes to the Mormon temple ceremony." *lds-mormon.com*. Accessed April 2, 2020. http://www.lds-mormon.com/whytemplechanges.shtml.

"Baptism for the Dead." *The Church of Jesus Christ of Latter-day Saints*. Accessed April 4, 2020. https://newsroom.churchofjesuschrist.org/article/baptism-for-the-dead.

"Baptisms for the Dead." *The Church of Jesus Christ of Latter-day Saints*. Accessed April 5, 2020. https://www.churchofjesuschrist.org/study/manual/gospel-topics/baptisms-for-the-dead.

"Bartholomew Gosnold." *Wikipedia, The Free Encyclopedia*. Last modified November 27, 2019. https://en.wikipedia.org/wiki/Bartholomew_Gosnold.

"Biblical Hebrew." *Wikipedia, The Free Encyclopedia*. Last modified April 6, 2020. https://en.wikipedia.org/wiki/Biblical_Hebrew.

"Border Security." *Department of Homeland Security*. Last modified February 25, 2019. https://www.dhs.gov/topic/border-security.

"Brigham Young." *Wikipedia, The Free Encyclopedia*. Last modified March 25, 2020. https://en.wikipedia.org/wiki/Brigham_Young.

"Britain and the Slave Trade." *The National Archives* (UK). Accessed March 28, 2020. http://www.nationalarchives.gov.uk/slavery/pdf/britain-and-the-trade.pdf.

"Chernobyl Accident 1986." *World Nuclear Association*. Last modified March 2020. https://www.world-nuclear.org/information-library/safety-and-security/safety-of-plants/chernobyl-accident.aspx.

"Christopher Columbus." *Wikipedia, The Free Encyclopedia*. Last modified March 28, 2020. https://en.wikipedia.org/wiki/Christopher_Columbus.

"Church Introduces Simplified Tithing, Donations Recording System." *The Church of Jesus Christ of Latter-day Saints*. Accessed March 31, 2020. https://www.churchofjesuschrist.org/study/ensign/1982/01/news-of-the-church/church-introduces-simplified-tithing-donations-recording-system.

"Church Supports Principles of *Utah Compact* on Immigration." *The Church of Jesus Christ of Latter-day Saints*. November 11, 2010. https://newsroom.churchofjesuschrist.org/article/church-supports-principles-of-utah-compact-on-immigration.

"City Creek Center Opens." *The Church of Jesus Christ of Latter-day Saints*. March 22, 2012. https://newsroom.churchofjesuschrist.org/article/city-creek-center-an-economic-revitalization.

"City Creek Center." *Wikipedia, The Free Encyclopedia*. Last modified January 8, 2020. https://en.wikipedia.org/wiki/City_Creek_Center.

"Cognitive dissonance." *Wikipedia, The Free Encyclopedia*. Last modified March 29, 2020. https://en.wikipedia.org/wiki/Cognitive_dissonance.

"Community of Christ." *Wikipedia, The Free Encyclopedia*. Last modified January 20, 2020. https://en.wikipedia.org/wiki/Community_of_Christ.

"Coronavirus disease 2019. *Wikipedia, The Free Encyclopedia*. Last modified April 6, 2020. https://en.wikipedia.org/wiki/Coronavirus_disease_2019.

"Coronavirus." *World Health Organization*. WHO. Accessed March 29, 2020. https://www.who.int/health-topics/coronavirus#tab=tab_1.

"Dead Sea Scrolls." *Wikipedia, The Free Encyclopedia*. Last modified March 29, 2020. https://en.wikipedia.org/wiki/Dead_Sea_Scrolls.

"Denouement." *Merriam-Webster Dictionary*. Accessed April 4, 2020. https://www.merriam-webster.com/dictionary/denouement.

"Divine Revelation in Modern Times." *The Church of Jesus Christ of Latter-day Saints*. December 12, 2011. https://newsroom.churchofjesuschrist.org/article/divine-revelation-modern-times.

"Does the Real Illuminati™ have anything to do with COVID-19?" *Real Illuminati™*. Accessed April 5, 2020. https://www.realilluminati.org/faq-s.

"Ethan Allen." *Wikipedia, The Free Encyclopedia*. Last modified March 25, 2020. https://en.wikipedia.org/wiki/Ethan_Allen.

"Facts and Statistics." *The Church of Jesus Christ of Latter-day Saints*. Accessed April 6, 2020. https://newsroom.churchofjesuschrist.org/facts-and-statistics.

"FamilySearch." *The Church of Jesus Christ of Latter-day Saints*. Accessed April 2, 2020. https://www.familysearch.org/en/.

"First Presidency Statement on Temples (Official Statement)." *The Church of Jesus Christ of Latter-day Saints. January 2,* 2019. https://newsroom.churchofjesuschrist.org/article/temple-worship.

"Fleeing For Our Lives: Central American Migrant Crisis." *Amnesty International*. Accessed March 29, 2020. https://www.amnestyusa.org/fleeing-for-our-lives-central-american-migrant-crisis/.

"Freemasonry." *Wikipedia, The Free Encyclopedia*. Last modified March 20, 2020. https://en.wikipedia.org/wiki/Freemasonry.

"Genealogy." *Church of Jesus Christ of Latter-day Saints*. Accessed March 29, 2020. https://newsroom.churchofjesuschrist.org/topic/genealogy.

"George Fox." *Wikipedia, The Free Encyclopedia*. Last modified March 11, 2020. https://en.wikipedia.org/wiki/George_Fox.

"George Washington's Masonic Apron on View." *Mount Vernon Ladies' Association*. Accessed April 3, 2020. https://www.mountvernon.org/plan-your-visit/calendar/exhibitions/george-washington-s-masonic-apron-on-view/.

"God in Islam." *Wikipedia, The Free Encyclopedia*. Last modified April 4, 2020. https://en.wikipedia.org/wiki/God_in_Islam.

"Hebrew language." *Encyclopædia Britannica*. Last modified November 16, 2018. https://www.britannica.com/print/article/259061.

"Hebrew language." *Wikipedia, The Free Encyclopedia*. Last modified March 31, 2020. https://en.wikipedia.org/wiki/Hebrew_language.

"HOPE For America's Future." *The Humanity Party®* (*THumP®*). 2017. https://www.humanityparty.com.

"How are plagues, like the current COVID-19, good for humanity?" *Real Illuminati™*. Accessed April 7, 2020. https://www.realilluminati.org/faq-s.

"How Slavery Helped Build a World Economy." *National Geographic*. January 3, 2003. https://www.nationalgeographic.com/news/2003/1/how-slavery-helped-build-a-world-economy/.

"Howard Zinn." *Wikipedia, The Free Encyclopedia*. Last modified March 29, 2020. https://en.wikipedia.org/wiki/Howard_Zinn.

"Hypocritical," *Merriam-Webster Dictionary*. Accessed April 4, 2020. https://www.merriam-webster.com/dictionary/hypocritically.

"Hyrum Smith." *Wikipedia, The Free Encyclopedia*. Last modified December 13, 2019. https://en.wikipedia.org/wiki/Hyrum_Smith.

"Immigration: Church Issues New Statement." *The Church of Jesus Christ of Latter-day Saints*. June 10, 2011. https://newsroom.churchofjesuschrist.org/article/immigration-church-issues-new-statement.

"Industrial Revolution." *Wikipedia, The Free Encyclopedia*. Last modified April 6, 2020. https://en.wikipedia.org/wiki/Industrial_Revolution.

"International Monetary Fund." *Wikipedia, The Free Encyclopedia*. Last modified March 29, 2020. https://en.wikipedia.org/wiki/International_Monetary_Fund.

"Jewish History." *Wikipedia, The Free Encyclopedia*. Last modified April 5, 2020. https://en.wikipedia.org/wiki/Jewish_history.

"Joseph F. Smith." *Wikipedia, The Free Encyclopedia*. Last modified February 28, 2020. https://en.wikipedia.org/wiki/Joseph_F._Smith.

"Joseph Fielding Smith." *Wikipedia, The Free Encyclopedia*. Last modified March 11, 2020. https://en.wikipedia.org/wiki/Joseph_Fielding_Smith.

"Joseph Smith." *Wikipedia, The Free Encyclopedia*. Last modified March 26, 2020. https://en.wikipedia.org/wiki/Joseph_Smith.

"List of suicides." *Wikipedia, The Free Encyclopedia*. Last modified April 4, 2020. https://en.wikipedia.org/wiki/List_of_suicides.

"List of wealthiest organizations." *Wikipedia, The Free Encyclopedia*. Last modified March 20, 2020. https://en.wikipedia.org/wiki/List_of_wealthiest_organizations#Religious_organizations.

"Lost Manuscript of the Book of Mormon." *The Church of Jesus Christ of Latter-day Saints*. Accessed April 5, 2020. https://www.churchofjesuschrist.org/study/history/topics/lost-manuscript-of-the-book-of-mormon.

"Memorandum." *The Humanity Party® Board of Directors in collaboration with The Marvelous Work and a Wonder®.* Accessed March 29, 2020. https://humanityparty.com/press_conference/05_28_18/Memorandum.pdf.

"Moors." *Wikipedia, The Free Encyclopedia.* Last modified April 4, 2020. https://en.wikipedia.org/wiki/Moors.

"Mormonism and polygamy." *Wikipedia, The Free Encyclopedia.* Last modified March 31, 2020. https://en.wikipedia.org/wiki/Mormonism_and_polygamy.

"Motives for the September 11 attacks. *Wikipedia, The Free Encyclopedia.* Last modified April 5, 2020. https://en.wikipedia.org/wiki/Motives_for_the_September_11_attacks.

"Nefarious." *Macmillan English Dictionary.* Accessed April 4, 2020. https://www.macmillandictionary.com/dictionary/american/nefarious#nefarious_3.

"Nuclear and radiation accidents and incidents." *Wikipedia, The Free Encyclopedia.* Last modified March 18, 2020. https://en.wikipedia.org/wiki/Nuclear_and_radiation_accidents_and_incidents.

"Nuclear explosion." *Wikipedia, The Free Encyclopedia.* Last modified March 28, 2020. https://en.wikipedia.org/wiki/Nuclear_explosion.

"Nuclear power." *Wikipedia, The Free Encyclopedia.* Last modified March 19, 2020. https://en.wikipedia.org/wiki/Nuclear_power.

"One Race, One People, One World—The Humanity Party®." *Real Illuminati™.* 2019. https://www.realilluminati.org.

"Online Donations—United States." *The Church of Jesus Christ of Latter-day Saints.* January 7, 2020. https://www.churchofjesuschrist.org/help/support/finance/online-donations.

"Ordinances." *The Church of Jesus Christ of Latter-day Saints.* Accessed March 29, 2020. https://www.churchofjesuschrist.org/study/manual/gospel-topics/ordinances.

"Patriotwritr." "America the Beautiful (performed by the Mormon Tabernacle Choir)." *YouTube.* December 3, 2008. https://www.youtube.com/watch?v=Rzs52OzgWOs.

"Penalty (Mormonism)." *Wikipedia, The Free Encyclopedia.* Last modified October 15, 2019. https://en.wikipedia.org/wiki/Penalty_(Mormonism).

"Plural Marriage and Families in Early Utah." *The Church of Jesus Christ of Latter-day Saints.* Accessed April 2, 2020. https://www.churchofjesuschrist.org/topics/plural-marriage-and-families-in-early-utah.

"Posthumous." *Macmillan English Dictionary.* Accessed April 4, 2020. https://www.macmillandictionary.com/dictionary/american/posthumous#posthumous_3.

"Preamble, We the People." *Interactive Constitution.* Accessed March 29, 2020. https://constitutioncenter.org/interactive-constitution/preamble.

"Priestcraft." *Collins English Dictionary.* Accessed April 4, 2020. https://www.collinsdictionary.com/dictionary/english/priestcraft.

"Psyche." *Macmillan English Dictionary.* Accessed March 29, 2020. https://www.macmillandictionary.com/us/dictionary/american/psyche.

"Question: Why were 'penalties' removed from the endowment?" *FairMormon.* Accessed April 5, 2020. https://www.fairmormon.org/answers/Mormonism_and_temples/Endowment/The_ordinance_versus_the_ritual_used_to_present_the_ordinance#Question:_Why_were_.22penalties.22_removed_from_the_Endowment.3F.

"Redemption of the Dead." *The Church of Jesus Christ of Latter-day Saints.* Accessed April 1, 2020. https://www.churchofjesuschrist.org/study/manual/foundations-of-the-restoration-teacher-material-2019/lesson-19-class-preparation-material-redemption-of-the-dead.

"Remember the Mission of the Church." *The Church of Jesus Christ of Latter-day Saints*. April 3, 1982. https://www.churchofjesuschrist.org/study/general-conference/1982/04/remember-the-mission-of-the-church.

"Sell out." *Merriam-Webster Dictionary*. Accessed April 4, 2020. https://www.merriam-webster.com/dictionary/sells.

"September 11 attacks." *Wikipedia, The Free Encyclopedia*. Last modified March 21, 2020. https://en.wikipedia.org/wiki/September_11_attacks.

"Shia Islam." *Wikipedia, The Free Encyclopedia*. Last modified March 29, 2020. https://en.wikipedia.org/wiki/Shia_Islam.

"Solar storm of 1859." *Wikipedia, The Free Encyclopedia*. Last modified March 20, 2020. https://en.wikipedia.org/wiki/Solar_storm_of_1859.

"Subjective (adjective)." Accessed April 6, 2020. https://www.merriam-webster.com/dictionary/subjective.

"Succession crisis (Latter Day Saints)." Last modified February 19, 2020. https://en.wikipedia.org/wiki/Succession_crisis_(Latter_Day_Saints).

"Teacher of Righteousness." *Wikipedia, The Free Encyclopedia*. Last modified January 31, 2020. https://en.wikipedia.org/wiki/Teacher_of_Righteousness.

"Temple Endowment." *The Church of Jesus Christ of Latter-day Saints*. Accessed April 6, 2020. https://www.churchofjesuschrist.org/study/history/topics/temple-endowment.

"Temple Penalties and Blood Oaths." *LDS-Mormon.com*. Accessed April 5, 2020. http://www.lds-mormon.com/veilworker/penalty.shtml.

"The Book of Lehi." *Real Illuminati™*. Accessed March 29, 2020. https://www.realilluminati.org/the-book-of-lehi.

"The Book of Malachi." *Real Illuminati™*. Accessed March 29, 2020. https://www.realilluminati.org/the-book-of-malachi.

"The Cause and Effect of Capitalism and Socialism on Humanity." *The Humanity Party®*. February 11, 2018. https://voicehumanity.tumblr.com/post/170751913294/the-battle-for-venezuela.

"The Church of Jesus Christ of Latter-day Saints." *The Church of Jesus Christ of Latter-day Saints*. Accessed March 29, 2020. https://www.churchofjesuschrist.org.

"The Church of Jesus Christ of Latter-day Saints." *Wikipedia, The Free Encyclopedia*. Last modified April 1, 2020. https://en.wikipedia.org/wiki/The_Church_of_Jesus_Christ_of_Latter-day_Saints.

"The Church of Jesus Christ." *The Church of Jesus Christ of Latter-day Saints*. Accessed April 5, 2020. https://www.churchofjesuschrist.org/church/organization/the-church-of-jesus-christ.

"The Constitution of The United People of the Republic of America." *The Humanity Party®*. Accessed March 29, 2020. https://humanityparty.com/proposed-constitution.

"The Dream of Mortal Life." *Real Illuminati™*. Accessed March 29, 2020. https://www.realilluminati.org/dream-of-mortal-life.

"The Humanity Party® Political Platform." *The Humanity Party®*. 2017. https://humanityparty.com/thump-platform.

"The Humanity Party®'s Plan to Eliminate Worldwide Poverty Explained!" The Humanity Party®. September 17, 2016. https://www.youtube.com/watch?v=kQ_Rlm_pC_k.

"The Jamestown Chronicles Timeline." *The Jamestown Chronicles*. 2007. https://www.historyisfun.org/sites/jamestown-chronicles/timeline.html.

"The Law of Tithing." in *Teachings of Presidents of the Church: Howard W. Hunter* (Salt Lake City: The Church of Jesus Christ of Latter-day Saints, 2015). Accessed March 29, 2020. https://www.churchofjesuschrist.org/study/manual/teachings-of-presidents-of-the-church-howard-w-hunter/chapter-9-the-law-of-tithing.

"The LDS Endowment." *ldsendowment.org*. Accessed March 29, 2020. http://www.ldsendowment.org/paralleltelestial.html.

"The Leon Levy Dead Sea Scrolls Digital Library | Discovery and Publication." *Israel Antiquities Authority*. Accessed April 6, 2020. https://www.deadseascrolls.org.il/learn-about-the-scrolls/discovery-and-publication?locale=en_US.

"The Man From Joe's Bar and Grill, The Autobiography of Christopher Marc Nemelka." *Real Illuminati™*. Accessed April 2, 2020. https://www.realilluminati.org/the-man-from-joe-s-bar-and-grill.

"The New Colossus." *Wikipedia, The Free Encyclopedia*. Last modified March 13, 2020. http://en.wikipedia.org/wiki/The_New_Colossus.

"The Plan of Salvation." *The Church of Jesus Christ of Latter-day Saints*. March 29, 2020. https://www.churchofjesuschrist.org/study/manual/preach-my-gospel-a-guide-to-missionary-service/lesson-2-the-plan-of-salvation.

"The Spartan Family. *HistoryWiz*. Accessed March 24, 2020. http://historywiz.com/didyouknow/spartanfamily.htm.

"Thomas Paine." *Wikipedia, The Free Encyclopedia*. Last modified March 29, 2020. https://en.wikipedia.org/wiki/Thomas_Paine.

"Timeline." *ldsendowment.org*. Accessed April 6, 2020. http://www.ldsendowment.org/timeline.html.

"Torah." *Wikipedia, The Free Encyclopedia*. Last modified March 19, 2020. https://en.wikipedia.org/wiki/Torah#Greek.

"Ultranationalism." *Wikipedia, The Free Encyclopedia*. Last modified April 4, 2020. https://en.wikipedia.org/wiki/Ultranationalism.

"United States Capitol." *Wikipedia, The Free Encyclopedia*. Last modified March 29, 2020. https://en.wikipedia.org/wiki/United_States_Capitol.

"Vegetation: Its Role in Weather and Climate." *North Carolina Climate Office*. Accessed March 29, 2020. https://climate.ncsu.edu/edu/Vegetation.

"Warfare in the Book of Mormon." *FairMormon*. Accessed April 6, 2020. https://www.fairmormon.org/answers/Book_of_Mormon/Warfare.

"What is the purpose of the Real Illuminati™?" *under* "Frequently Asked Questions." *Real Illuminati™*. Accessed April 4, 2020. https://www.realilluminati.org/faq-s.

"World Bank." *Wikipedia, The Free Encyclopedia*. Last modified March 27, 2020. https://en.wikipedia.org/wiki/World_Bank.

"World War II." *Wikipedia, The Free Encyclopedia*. Last modified March 20, 2020. https://en.wikipedia.org/wiki/World_War_II.

"Wyoming Territory." *Wikipedia, The Free Encyclopedia*. Last modified March 28, 2020. https://en.wikipedia.org/wiki/Wyoming_Territory.

A. Dupont-Sommer. *The Dead Sea Scrolls*. Oxford: Basil Blackwell, 1952.

Alice Hines. "City Creek, Mormon Shopping Mall, Boasts Flame-Shooting Fountains, Biblical Splendor (Photos)." *HuffPost*. March 22, 2012. https://www.huffpost.com/entry/city-creek-mormon-mall_n_1372695.

Anonymous. *Human Reality—Who We Are and Why We Exist!* Melba: Worldwide United, 2009.

Asma Afsaruddin. "Allah." *Encyclopedia Britannica*. Last modified September 16, 2019. https://www.britannica.com/topic/Allah.

B. H. Roberts, *History of the Church of Jesus Christ of Latter-day Saints. An Introduction and notes by B. H. Roberts. Seven Volumes*. Salt Lake City: Deseret Book, 1980. Nicknamed *Documentary History of the Church* or *DHC*, https://archive.org/details/HistoryOfTheChurchhcVolumes1-7original1902EditionPdf/mode/2up.

BMC Team. "Why are There So Many War Chapters in the Book of Mormon?" *Book of Mormon Central*. August 3, 2016. https://knowhy.bookofmormoncentral.org/knowhy/why-are-there-so-many-war-chapters-in-the-book-of-mormon.

Bonnie Hoffman. "Six Aristotelian Elements of a Play." *Bellevue College*. Accessed April 4, 2020. https://www2.bellevuecollege.edu/artshum/materials/drama/Hoffman/101SIXARISTOAPLAYspr03.asp.

Brigham Young. *Journal of Discourses*. Volume 11. Liverpool: B. Young, June 1867.

Bruce D. Porter. "Building the Kingdom." *The Church of Jesus Christ of Latter-day Saints*. April 1, 2001. https://www.churchofjesuschrist.org/study/general-conference/2001/04/building-the-kingdom.

Bruce R. McConkie. "Polygamy," in *Mormon Doctrine*. 2nd ed. Salt Lake City: Bookcraft, 1966. https://archive.org/details/MormonDoctrine1966/page/n413/mode/2up.

Cari Nierenberg. "Rich Kids and Drugs: Addiction May Hit Wealthy Students Hardest." June 1, 2017. https://www.livescience.com/59329-drug-alcohol-addiction-wealthy-students.html.

Caroline Winter, Katherine Burton, Nick Tamasi and Anita Kumar. "The money behind the Mormon message." *Bloomberg Businessweek*. October 5, 2012. *The Salt Lake Tribune*. https://archive.sltrib.com/article.php?id=54478720&itype=cmsid.

Chris Henrichsen. "A New Mission: Caring for the Poor and the Needy." *Faith-Promoting Rumor* (blog). December 6, 2009. http://faithpromotingrumor.com/2009/12/06/a-new-mission-caring-and-the-poor-and-the-needy.

Christopher. "Facebook Live video." December 20, 2016.

———. "Jewish & LDS (Mormon) Parallels." *Marvelous Work and a Wonder®*. 2010. www.pearlpublishing.net/tsp/download/JewishLDSParallels.4.4.20.pdf.

———. "Letter to The First Presidency of the Church of Jesus Christ of Latter-day Saints," in *TSP*. Worldwide United, 2008. www.pearlpublishing.net/tsp/download/TSP_Secured.pdf.

———. *666, The Mark of America—Seat of the Beast: The Apostle John's New Testament Revelation Unfolded*. Worldwide United, 2006. https://www.realilluminati.org/666-mark-of-america.

———. *Sacred, not Secret—The [Authorized and] Official Guide In Understanding the LDS Temple Endowment*. Melba: Worldwide United, 2008. https://www.realilluminati.org/sacred-not-secret.

———. *Without Disclosing My True Identity—The Authorized and Official Biography of the Mormon Prophet, Joseph Smith, Jr.* Melba: Worldwide United, 2012. https://www.realilluminati.org/without-disclosing-my-true-identity.

Committee on Masonic Education. "Masonic Questions & Answers." *subtopic* "American Masonic History." *Grand Lodge of Pennsylvania*. Accessed March 29, 2020. https://pagrandlodge.org/masonic-q-and-a/.

Cynthia Vinney. "Freud: Id, Ego, and Superego Explained." *ThoughtCo*. February 28, 2019. https://www.thoughtco.com/id-ego-and-superego-4582342.

Dallin H. Oaks. "The Only True and Living Church." *The Church of Jesus Christ of Latter-day Saints*. June 25, 2010. https://www.churchofjesuschrist.org/study/new-era/2011/08/the-only-true-and-living-church.

Daniel Gonzalez. "The 2019 migrant surge is unlike any we've seen before. This is why." *USA Today*. September 25, 2019. https://www.usatoday.com/in-depth/news/nation/2019/09/23/immigration-issues-migrants-mexico-central-america-caravans-smuggling/2026215001/.

Dennis Lythgoe. "Utah Statehood." *Deseret News*. February 8, 1996. https://www.deseret.com/1996/2/8/19223925/utah-statehood.

E.J. Mundell. "Antidepressant use in U.S. soars by 65 percent in 15 years." *CBS News*. August 16, 2017. https://www.cbsnews.com/news/antidepressant-use-soars-65-percent-in-15-years/.

Editorial Staff. "Addiction among Socioeconomic Groups." *American Addiction Centers*. June 20, 2019. https://sunrisehouse.com/addiction-demographics/socioeconomic-groups.

Edwin M. Yamauchi. "The Teacher of Righteousness from Qumran and Jesus of Nazareth." *Christianity Today* 10, no. 16 (May 13, 1966): 12. https://www.christianitytoday.com/ct/1966/may-13/teacher-of-righteousness-from-qumran-and-jesus-of-nazareth.html.

EJ Dickson. "Prayer, Politics and Power: 'The Family' Reveals Our Insidious American Theocracy." *RollingStone*. August 9, 2019. https://www.rollingstone.com/culture/culture-features/netflix-the-family-jesse-moss-secret-christian-cult-washington-dc-869396/.

Eric Eustice Williams. *Capitalism and Slavery*. Chapel Hill: UNC Press, 1944. https://archive.org/details/capitalismandsla033027mbp/page/n8/mode/2up.

Fred Gladstone Bratton. *A History of the Bible*. Boston: Beacon Press, 1967.

Geza Vermes. *The Complete Dead Sea Scrolls in English (Revised Edition)*. London: Penguin Books, 2004. https://epdf.pub/queue/the-complete-dead-sea-scrolls-in-english.html.

Gramps. "Polygamy in the millennium." *Ask Gramps*. April 23, 2011. https://askgramps.org/polygamy-in-the-millenium/.

Harold Hancock. "Is There a Difference Between Hebrews, Jews and Israelites?" *Timberland Drive church of Christ*. Accessed April 6, 2020. https://www.timberlandchurch.org/articles/is-there-a-difference-between-hebrews-jews-and-israelites.

Henry B. Eyring. "Families Can Be Together Forever." *Church of Jesus Christ of Latter-day Saints*. June 2015. https://www.churchofjesuschrist.org/study/ensign/2015/06/families-can-be-together-forever.

———. "The Lord Leads His Church." *The Church of Jesus Christ of Latter-day Saints*. September 30, 2017. https://www.churchofjesuschrist.org/study/general-conference/2017/10/the-lord-leads-his-church.

———. "The True and Living Church." *The Church of Jesus Christ of Latter-day Saints*. April 5, 2008. https://www.churchofjesuschrist.org/study/general-conference/2008/04/the-true-and-living-church.

History.com Editors. "Babylonia." *History.com*. Last modified August 20, 2019. https://www.history.com/topics/ancient-middle-east/babylonia.

History.com Editors. "Revolutionary War." *History.com*. Last modified September 3, 2019. https://www.history.com/topics/american-revolution/american-revolution-history.

Howard W. Hunter. "Your Temple Recommend." *The Church of Jesus Christ of Latter-day Saints*. Accessed March 31, 2020. https://www.churchofjesuschrist.org/study/new-era/1995/04/your-temple-recommend.

Howard Zinn. *The People's History of the United States of America*. New York: Harper Perennial Modern Classics, 2005. https://www.historyisaweapon.com/zinnapeopleshistory.html.

Jason Williams. "The Gift." *The George Washington Masonic Cave*. November 26, 2018. https://georgewashingtoncave.org/2018/11/26/the-gift/.

Jeffrey R. Holland. "God's Words Never Cease: The Bible, the Book of Mormon, and Continuing Revelation." *The Church of Jesus Christ of Latter-day Saints*. July 14, 2009. https://www.churchofjesuschrist.org/media-library/video/2009-07-29-gods-words-never-cease.

———. "God's Words Never Cease: The Bible, the Book of Mormon, and Continuing Revelation." *The Church of Jesus Christ of Latter-day Saints*. July 14, 2009. https://www.youtube.com/watch?v=K_xl_AR0IRs.

John A. Widtsoe. *Priesthood and Church Government*. Salt Lake City: Deseret Book, 1939.

John Dart. "Mormons Modify Temple Rites: Ceremony: Woman's vow to obey husband is dropped. Changes are called most significant since 1978." *Los Angeles Times*: May 5, 1990. https://www.latimes.com/archives/la-xpm-1990-05-05-vw-353-story.html.

Joseph Smith, Junior, Author and Proprietor. *The Book of Mormon—An Account Written by the Hand of Mormon, Upon Plates Taken from the Plates of Nephi*. Palmyra: E. B. Grandin, 1830. Including "The Testimony of Three Witnesses" (Oliver Cowdery, David Whitmer, and Martin Harris).

Julie Cart. "Study Finds Utah Leads Nation in Antidepressant Use. *LA Times*. February 20, 2002. https://www.latimes.com/archives/la-xpm-2002-feb-20-mn-28924-story.html.

Lauren Morello. "Cutting Down Rainforests Also Cuts Down on Rainfall." *Scientific American*. September 6, 2012. https://www.scientificamerican.com/article/cutting-down-rainforests/.

Leslie Kramer. "Mercantilism and the Colonies of Great Britain." *Investopedia*. June 26, 2019. https://www.investopedia.com/ask/answers/041615/how-did-mercantilism-affect-colonies-great-britain.asp.

M. Russell Ballard. "The True, Pure, and Simple Gospel of Jesus Christ." *The Church of Jesus Christ of Latter-day Saints*. April 6, 2019. https://www.churchofjesuschrist.org/study/general-conference/2019/04/23ballard.

Maggie Fox. "One in 6 Americans Take Antidepressants, Other Psychiatric Drugs: Study." *NBC News*. December 12, 2016. https://www.nbcnews.com/health/health-news/one-6-americans-take-antidepressants-other-psychiatric-drugs-n695141.

Mark Cartwright. "Ancient Greek Theatre." *Ancient History Encyclopedia*. July 14, 2016. https://www.ancient.eu/Greek_Theatre/.

Mark E. Petersen. "Follow the Prophets." *The Church of Jesus Christ of Latter-day Saints*. October 4, 1981. https://www.churchofjesuschrist.org/study/general-conference/1981/10/follow-the-prophets.

Nat Berman. "20 Famous Actors Who Committed Suicide." *TVOvermind*. August 10, 2018. https://www.tvovermind.com/actors-who-committed-suicide.

Owen Jarus. "Biblical Battles: 12 Ancient Wars Lifted from the Bible." *Live Science*. July 24, 2017. https://www.livescience.com/59911-ancient-biblical-battles.html.

Parley P. Pratt. "Reminiscences of the Church in Nauvoo." *Millennial Star* 55, no. 36 (September 4, 1893): 584–6. https://contentdm.lib.byu.edu/digital/collection/MStar/id/19227/rec/55.

Paul C. Gutjahr. *Lives of Great Religious Books*. Princeton: Princeton Univ. Press, 2012. https://books.google.com/books?id=Mmz4Eob3MDkC.

Paul Glader. "Mormon Church Stockpiled $100 Billion Intended for Charities and Misled LDS Members, Whistleblower Says." *Newsweek* and *Religion Unplugged*. December 17, 2019. https://www.newsweek.com/mormon-church-stockpiled-100-billion-intended-charities-misled-lds-members-whistleblower-says-1477809.

Peggy Fletcher Stack and David Noyce. "LDS Church changes temple ceremony; faithful feminists will see revisions and additions as a 'leap forward'." *The Salt Lake Tribune*. January 3, 2019. https://www.sltrib.com/religion/2019/01/02/lds-church-releases/.

Peggy Fletcher Stack. "LDS Church kept the lid on its $100B fund for fear tithing receipts would fall, account boss tells Wall Street Journal." *The Salt Lake Tribune*. February 8, 2020. https://www.sltrib.com/news/2020/02/08/lds-church-kept-lid-its-b/.

———. "New LDS emphasis: Care for the needy." *The Salt Lake Tribune*. December 9, 2009. https://archive.sltrib.com/story.php?ref=/lds/ci_13965607.

Rebecca Onion. "America's Other Original Sin." *Slate*. January 18, 2016. http://www.slate.com/articles/news_and_politics/cover_story/2016/01/native_american_slavery_historians_uncover_a_chilling_chapter_in_u_s_history.html.

Richard G. Scott. "The Joy of Redeeming the Dead." *The Church of Jesus Christ of Latter-day Saints*. October 7, 2012. https://www.churchofjesuschrist.org/study/general-conference/2012/10/the-joy-of-redeeming-the-dead.

Russel[l] M. Nelson. "Vicarious Work for the Dead." *The Church of Jesus Christ of Latter-day Saints*. October 8, 2006. https://www.churchofjesuschrist.org/media-library/video/2012-06-2710-vicarious-work-for-the-dead.

Russell Goldman. "Two Studies Find Depression Widespread in Utah." *ABC News*. February 9, 2009. https://abcnews.go.com/Health/MindMoodNews/story?id=4403731&page=1.

Russell M. Nelson. "Sustaining the Prophets." *The Church of Jesus Christ of Latter-day Saints*. October 5, 2014. https://www.churchofjesuschrist.org/study/general-conference/2014/10/sustaining-the-prophets.

Salt Lake City Cemetery. 200 "N" Street, gravesite "Park 14-18-5E," denoting Park Plat, Section 14, Lot 8, Grave 5 East. Erected on June 16, 2010.

Saul McLeod. "Id, ego and superego." *Simply psychology*. September 25, 2019. https://www.simplypsychology.org/psyche.html.

Skye Gould and Lauren F Friedman. "Something startling is going on with antidepressant use around the world." *Business Insider*. February 4, 2016. https://www.businessinsider.com/countries-largest-antidepressant-drug-users-2016-2.

Stacy Johnson. "President Trump meets with LDS Church leadership at Welfare Square." *Daily Herald*. December 4, 2017. https://www.heraldextra.com/news/local/faith/president-trump-meets-with-lds-church-leadership-at-welfare-square/article_f049d6bd-7fff-5607-af43-2129af49b535.html.

The Doctrine and Covenants of The Church of Jesus Christ of Latter-day Saints. Salt Lake City: The Church of Jesus Christ of Latter-day Saints, 1986. *See specifically* "Official Declaration—1" (October 6, 1890) and "Official Declaration—2." (June 1, 1978).

The Pearl of Great Price. Salt Lake City: The Church of Jesus Christ of Latter-day Saints. 2013. Including "Joseph Smith—History" and "Articles of Faith."

The Real Illuminati™. "The Book of Mormon (1830 Edition)." *Real Illuminati*™. Accessed March 29, 2020. https://www.realilluminati.org/the-book-of-mormon.

——— *One People, One World, One Government*. Melba: Worldwide United, upcoming. https://www.realilluminati.org/one-people-one-world-one-goverment.

———. *The True History of Religion—How Religion Destroys the Human Race and What the Real Illuminati™ Has Attempted to do Through Religion to Save the Human Race.* Melba: Worldwide United, 2019. Large print edition. https://www.realilluminati.org/the-true-history-of-religion.

The Sealed Portion—The Final Testament of Jesus Christ. Translated by Christopher. 2nd ed. Worldwide United, 2008. Including "Appendix 2: The Book of Lehi, The Lost 116-Page Manuscript" and "Appendix 3: The First Vision." https://www.realilluminati.org/the-sealed-portion/.

ONE RACE,
ONE PEOPLE,
ONE WORLD

THE HUMANITY PARTY®

A NEW WORLD GOVERNMENT
Earth's only hope

HUMANITYPARTY.COM

CPSIA information can be obtained
at www.ICGtesting.com
Printed in the USA
BVHW011439110520
578439BV00005B/14